UP YOUR
VEGGIES

UP YOUR VEGGIES

Flexitarian Recipes for the Whole Family

TOBY AMIDOR

Robert
ROSE

Library and Archives Canada Cataloguing in Publication
Title: Up your veggies : flexitarian recipes for the whole family / Toby Amidor.
Names: Amidor, Toby, author.
Description: Includes index.
Identifiers: Canadiana 20230159486 | ISBN 9780778807131 (softcover)
Subjects: LCSH: Vegetarian cooking. | LCSH: Cooking (Vegetables) | LCGFT: Cookbooks.
Classification: LCC TX837 .A44 2023 | DDC 641.5/636—dc23

Disclaimer
The recipes in this book have been carefully tested by our kitchen and our tasters. To the best of our knowledge, they are safe and nutritious for ordinary use and users. For those people with food or other allergies, or who have special food requirements or health issues, please read the suggested contents of each recipe carefully and determine whether or not they may create a problem for you. All recipes are used at the risk of the consumer.

We cannot be responsible for any hazards, loss or damage that may occur as a result of any recipe use.

For those with special needs, allergies, requirements or health problems, in the event of any doubt, please contact your medical adviser prior to the use of any recipe.

At the time of publication, all URLs referenced link to existing websites. Robert Rose Inc. is not responsible for maintaining, and does not endorse the content of, any website or content not created by Robert Rose Inc.

EDITOR: Meredith Dees
COPYEDITOR & INDEXER: Gillian Watts
PROOFREADER: Kelly Jones
COVER & BOOK DESIGN: PageWave Graphics Inc.
COVER & INTERIOR PHOTOGRAPHY: Ashley Lima
FOOD & PROP STYLING: Ashley Lima
TEXTURE (PAGES 3, 7, 13, 31, 37, 55, 75, 95, 111, 151, 185, 193): © Getty Images

Published by Robert Rose Inc.
120 Eglinton Avenue East, Suite 800, Toronto, Ontario, Canada M4P 1E2
Tel: (416) 322-6552 Fax: (416) 322-6936
www.robertrose.ca

Printed and bound in China

1 2 3 4 5 6 7 8 9 ESP 31 30 29 28 27 26 25 24 23

To my three amazing children
Schoen, Ellena and Micah,
who are the lights of my life.
Keep eating those veggies!

CONTENTS

INTRODUCTION

How many times have you heard a parent tell their kids to eat their veggies? (Or, have you said it yourself?) Kids aren't the only problem, though: in the United States, only one in 10 adults meet the daily recommended vegetable intake, while in Canada, it's just three in 10 adults. Eating your vegetables daily can help provide your body with the nutrition it needs to thrive, plus research shows that it can help lower the risk of cardiovascular disease as well chronic diseases such as type 2 diabetes and cancer.

Vegetables also taste great! Different veggies can lend a range of flavors in many dishes, from sweet to savory to umami. Plus, the variety of colors makes dishes more visually appealing. Have you ever been told that people eat with their eyes? If you see something with a pretty color or that looks attractive, you are more likely to want to eat that food.

This purpose of this book is to encourage you to overcome popular barriers, like taste, cost and time, in order to eat more veggies. In this cookbook, you will find 100 delicious plant-forward recipes that use accessible ingredients and keep prep and cooking time in mind. Tips feature information about minimizing food waste to save you money, and I've highlighted recipes that take 30 minutes or less, are easy to meal-prep or are made in one pot.

However, vegetables aren't the only food that should be on your plate. I take a flexitarian approach to eating, which means adding lots of plants to your plate, but also leaving room for animal products. As a registered dietitian, I believe there is no reason you need to choose one type of protein over the other or pit foods against each other, especially plants versus animals. The reason is simple: to get the most nutrients and flavor from your meals, you should serve your veggies with starches, fruit, protein, healthy fat, milk and dairy foods or soy-milk beverages and soy yogurt. When you eat different foods at the same time throughout your day, it allows for better absorption of nutrients. For example, when you eat spinach that is flavored with lemon juice, the vitamin C from the lemon juice helps the plant-based iron absorb more easily. Eating a wider variety of foods gives you more opportunities to take in the nutrients that your body needs to stay healthy. Some flexitarian diets recommend that 10 or 20 percent of your diet come from animal products, but in my opinion, that number is up to you.

Many of these recipes use plant-based foods like beans, peas, lentils, starches, nuts and seeds, or animal-based proteins like eggs, chicken, beef, pork, seafood and fish to complement the vegetables. I've also provided recommendations for protein substitutions throughout the book, so you can always customize recipes to your preferences. For example, if you want to swap chicken for tofu, then go for it! Just be mindful that it may change the cooking time.

This cookbook is truly a celebration of vegetables — their delicious flavors, gorgeous colors and important contributions to overall health. Take the time to enjoy shopping for your vegetables in the produce aisle and when selecting them online: don't be afraid to try something new. And it doesn't matter which type of vegetables you choose — whether they are organic, conventional, local or ugly. Be proud of the food you put on your plate and look for opportunities in your day to get more.

This book was made to be enjoyed by you any way you wish. Hopefully, it will help you to improve your health, and up your veggies and your recipe repertoire, too.

Happy, healthy cooking!

Toby
xxx

CHAPTER 1

CELEBRATING VEGETABLES

In this chapter we will explore the different groups of vegetables, the health benefits of vegetables, and how vegetables can fit onto your plate.

A LOOK AT VEGETABLES

When it comes to vegetables, there is a reason why many dietitians recommend eating a rainbow of colors. Each color grouping of veggies provides different nutrients. There is a chart on the next page outlining the five vegetable groups, which vegetables are in each group, and the many important nutrients that each provides.

VEGETABLE GROUPS	EXAMPLES	IMPORTANT NUTRIENTS	SAMPLE RECIPES
Dark Green Vegetables	Arugula, broccoli, escarole, green leafy lettuce, kale, mesclun, spinach, Swiss chard, romaine	• Calcium • Carotenoids • Fiber • Folate • Iron • Vitamin C • Vitamin K	• All Greens Salad with Lemon Vinaigrette (page 122) • Broccoli Cheddar Soup (page 82) • Peach Spinach Smoothie (page 50)
Red and Orange Vegetables	Carrot, butternut squash, pumpkin, red and orange bell pepper, sweet potato, tomato	• Beta-carotene (vitamin A) • Potassium • Vitamin C • Vitamin K	• Carrot Salad with Raisins and Apples (page 121) • Roasted Red Pepper Deviled Eggs (page 71) • Tomato and White Bean Quinoa Bowls (page 156)
Beans, Peas and Lentils	Black bean, black-eyed (cow) pea or split pea, fava bean, garbanzo bean (chickpeas), kidney bean, lima bean, mung bean, navy bean, pigeon pea, pinto bean, lentil (red, brown and green), soybean	• Fiber • Folate • Iron • Potassium • Protein • Zinc	• Avocado and White Bean Sandwich (page 99) • Flank Steak Bowls with Black Beans, Peppers and Onions (page 179) • Split Pea Soup with Ham and Barley (page 93)
Starchy Vegetables	Breadfruit, cassava, corn, jicama, parsnip, plantain, white potato, water chestnut, yam, yucca	• Carbohydrates • Fiber • Potassium • Vitamin C	• Chicken, Rice and Root Vegetable Soup (page 81) • Twice-Baked Potatoes with the Works (page 64)
Other Vegetables	Asparagus, beet, Brussels sprout, cabbage, cauliflower, celery, cucumber, eggplant, green bean, kohlrabi, mushroom, okra, onion, radish, rutabaga, snow pea, summer squash, tomatillo, turnip	• A wide variety of nutrients (depending on the vegetable), including fiber, vitamins and minerals	• Eggplant Caponata (page 72) • Farro and Mushroom Bowls with Flounder (page 164) • Red Cabbage Slaw with Mandarins and Almonds (page 112)

It doesn't matter if you choose fresh, canned or frozen vegetables — all count toward your recommended daily intake. In addition, you'll find essential nutrients in all these forms, though the quantities do vary slightly. For example, sometimes a canned form of the vegetable has more of a nutrient than the fresh form (tomatoes come to mind; see page 24). Also, when you choose canned vegetables, be mindful of their sodium content; draining and rinsing can help decrease the amount of sodium in each product. When buying frozen vegetables, look for those without sauces or added saturated fat such as butter.

THE HEALTH BENEFITS OF VEGETABLES

There are many benefits to getting enough veggies every day. Veggies of all colors are filled with vitamins, minerals, antioxidants and phytonutrients (natural plant compounds that help prevent or fight disease). For example, vitamin C helps fight infections and heal wounds. Other health benefits of vegetables include:

- **DECREASED BLOOD PRESSURE:** Leafy green veggies such as kale and spinach provide potassium, as do potatoes. Potassium helps your kidneys filter sodium out of your body, which can help reduce blood pressure.

- **DECREASED RISK OF HEART DISEASE:** Green leafy veggies also provide vitamin K. This vitamin is thought to help lower the risk of damage to your arteries and help prevent calcium from building up in them, which could cause a blockage.

- **BETTER DIGESTIVE HEALTH:** Veggies contain fiber, a type of carbohydrate that isn't broken down or absorbed but rather passes through your digestive system. Getting enough fiber helps keep your digestive system healthy, decrease the risk of colon cancer and alleviate constipation.

- **BETTER BLOOD SUGAR CONTROL FOR PEOPLE WITH DIABETES:** The fiber from veggies can slow how quickly sugar is absorbed into the body, which can help control spikes in blood sugar after eating. This is especially true for low-carb veggies such as kale, spinach, asparagus, mushrooms, broccoli, cauliflower and cucumbers.

- **IMPROVED MOOD:** Researchers from Australia have found that eating more veggies and fruit makes people happier.

SHOULD YOU CHOOSE ORGANIC VEGETABLES?

As a dietitian, I frequently get asked about eating organic veggies. However, this is a personal choice. Research shows that there is no major nutritional difference between organic and conventional produce. There are several organizations that push for organic veggies and disparage conventional ones for having high amounts of pesticide residue. However, in the United States, the pesticide levels found in veggies are well below the Food and Drug Administration (FDA) maximums. For example, in one day you would need to eat 774 servings of spinach — considered by consumer advocacy groups to contain higher residues — to have any negative effects on your body, if any. Given that most folks in the United States and Canada do not consume enough veggies to begin with, eating any type of vegetable should be the priority to reap their benefits.

Organic produce is also quite expensive. Do not put pressure on yourself by thinking you need to spend more money. As a registered dietitian and the mom of several kids in college, I am certainly on a budget. I choose conventional veggies because I have to keep an eye on my food spending. Do what is best for you, and be proud of the veggies you put in your body!

THE TOP 15 VEGETABLES

Below you'll find info on the top veggies people like to eat, ones that appear frequently in this cookbook. For each vegetable, I've included nutritional information, shopping and storage tips, and recipes from this book that include them.

1 · ASPARAGUS

ASPARAGUS FACT: Asparagus contains a natural plant compound called asparagine, which gives this vegetable a diuretic effect. It's what can cause some folks to notice a weird odor from their urine after eating these green stalks.

NUTRITION LOWDOWN: Half a cup (125 mL) of cooked asparagus provides 19.8 calories, 2.16 grams of protein, 0.198 grams of fat, 3.7 grams of carbohydrates and 1.8 grams of fiber. It is also a good source of vitamin C.

SHOPPING AND STORAGE TIPS: Opt for fresh, frozen or canned asparagus. When buying fresh asparagus, look for bunches that are firm, straight and brightly colored. Check the tips, which should be tightly closed. Store fresh asparagus in the refrigerator in a plastic bag (reusable if possible) or upright in a container with 1 inch (2.5 cm) of water; use within 3 days. Fresh asparagus can be cooked and then frozen for up to 8 months.

RECIPE
- All Greens Salad with Lemon Vinaigrette (page 122)

2 · BELL PEPPERS

BELL PEPPER FACT: Bell peppers are the most popular sweet pepper sold. Their shape resembles a bell, which is how they got their name.

NUTRITION LOWDOWN: One medium green bell pepper provides 23.8 calories, 1.02 grams of protein, 0.2 grams of fat, 5.52 grams of carbohydrates and 2.02 grams of fiber. Peppers are high in vitamin C. They also contain an antioxidant called lycopene, which has been shown to help lower the risk of heart disease, prostate cancer and macular degeneration, an eye disease associated with aging.

SHOPPING AND STORAGE TIPS: Look for fresh, frozen or canned bell peppers. Choose fresh bell peppers that are firm, bright, shiny and heavy for their size. Avoid those with bruises and soft spots or peppers that are soft or shriveled. Store fresh bell peppers in a plastic bag (reusable if possible) in the refrigerator for up to 1 week.

SELECT RECIPES
- Ruby Red Smoothie (page 49)
- Greek Salad Skewers (page 59)
- Roasted Red Pepper Deviled Eggs (page 71)
- Eggplant Caponata (page 72)
- Tomato Cucumber Gazpacho (page 80)
- Roasted Vegetable Grilled Cheese (page 96)
- Mushroom Cheesesteak Sandwich (page 102)
- Veggie Chicken Salad Sandwich (page 105)
- Easy Cucumber Salad (page 115)
- Roasted Tomato and Shrimp Salad (page 132)
- Sautéed Chicken and Vegetable Bowls with Couscous (page 168)
- Unstuffed Pepper Bowls (page 176)
- Cajun-Flavored Vegetable and Andouille Sausage Bowls (page 183)
- Pineapple Salsa (page 188)

3 · BROCCOLI

BROCCOLI FACT: If broccoli isn't harvested at the right time, it will turn into a head of yellow flowers.

NUTRITION LOWDOWN: One cup (250 mL) of raw broccoli provides 29.6 calories, 1.95 grams of protein, 0.258 grams of fat, 2.89 grams of carbohydrates and 1.82 grams of fiber. It's also high in vitamin C and a good source of potassium.

SHOPPING AND STORAGE TIPS: Choose fresh or frozen broccoli. Look for fresh broccoli that is odorless and has tight bluish-green florets. Store in the refrigerator for up to 5 days.

RECIPES
- Broccoli Cheddar Soup (page 82)
- Broccoli Salad with Pepitas (page 117)
- Fried Rice Bowls with Broccoli and Cashews (page 157)
- Roasted Salmon Bowls with Mixed Vegetables (page 161)
- Sautéed Chicken and Vegetable Bowls with Couscous (page 168)
- Sweet-and-Sour Chicken Bowls with Broccoli and Peppers (page 171)
- Chicken and Steamed Veggie Bowls with Peanut Sauce (page 172)
- Cajun-Flavored Vegetable and Andouille Sausage Bowls (page 183)

4 · CARROTS

CARROT FACT: Carrots grow downward into the soil instead of upward toward the sun.

NUTRITION LOWDOWN: One medium fresh carrot provides 25.01 calories, 0.57 grams of protein, 1.71 grams of fat, 5.84 grams of carbohydrates and 1.71 grams of fiber. Carrots are high in vitamin C.

SHOPPING AND STORAGE TIPS: Choose fresh, frozen or canned carrots. When selecting fresh carrots, check that they are firm, smooth and crisp, with a deep color and fresh green tops. Avoid those that are soft, wilted or split. Store carrots, with the tops removed, in a plastic bag (reusable if possible) in the refrigerator for up to 2 weeks.

SELECT RECIPES

- Sunshine Smoothie (page 42)
- Roasted Carrot Hummus (page 63)
- Eggplant Caponata (page 72)
- Roasted Carrot Soup with Pesto (page 79)
- Udon Noodle and Shrimp Soup (page 89)
- Split Pea Soup with Ham and Barley (page 93)
- Veggie Chicken Salad Sandwich (page 105)
- Red Cabbage Slaw with Mandarins and Almonds (page 112)
- Kale and Carrot Salad (page 114)
- Soba Noodle Salad with Vegetables and Grilled Tofu (page 128)
- Brussels Sprouts, Kale and Farro Bowls (page 152)
- Poached Egg Superfood Bowls (page 158)
- Roasted Salmon Bowls with Mixed Vegetables (page 161)

5 · CAULIFLOWER

CAULIFLOWER FACT: Cauliflower is part of the cruciferous veggie family, along with cabbage, broccoli and mustard greens, among others.

NUTRITION LOWDOWN: One cup (250 mL) of chopped fresh cauliflower provides 50 calories, 2.49 grams of protein, 0.43 grams of fat, 10.81 grams of carbohydrates and 3.71 grams of fiber. It is also high in vitamin C.

SHOPPING AND STORAGE TIPS: Choose fresh or frozen cauliflower. When selecting fresh, look for cauliflower with compact, creamy-white curds and bright green leaves that are firmly attached. Avoid cauliflower that has brown spots or loose, separated sections. Store fresh cauliflower in a plastic bag (reusable if possible) in the refrigerator for up to 5 days.

RECIPES

- Cauliflower-Berry Smoothie (page 38)
- Chicken and Steamed Veggie Bowls with Peanut Sauce (page 172)

6 · CELERY

CELERY FACT: This veggie is 95 percent water.

NUTRITION LOWDOWN: One cup (250 mL) of fresh chopped celery provides 16.16 calories, 0.7 grams of protein, 0.17 grams of fat, 3 grams of carbohydrates and 1.62 grams of fiber. Celery is a good source of vitamin C.

SHOPPING AND STORAGE TIPS: Choose fresh celery with straight, firm stalks and bright green leaves. Avoid stalks that are woody or limp or have a musty odor. Store fresh celery in a plastic bag (reusable if possible) in the refrigerator for up to 1 week.

RECIPES

- Green Smoothie with Apple and Celery (page 45)
- Tuna-Filled Cucumber Boats (page 56)
- Eggplant Caponata (page 72)
- Chicken, Rice and Root Vegetable Soup (page 81)
- Broccoli Cheddar Soup (page 82)
- Split Pea Soup with Ham and Barley (page 93)
- Veggie Chicken Salad Sandwich (page 105)
- Bell Pepper Sandwich with Tuna (page 106)

7 · CORN

CORN FACT: Corn grows in a rainbow of colors: yellow, purple, white, brown and even multicolored. The two most popular types are white and yellow.

NUTRITION LOWDOWN: Half a cup (125 mL) of cooked corn kernels provides 50 calories, 2.49 grams of protein, 0.43 grams of fat, 16.04 grams of carbohydrates and 3.71 grams of fiber.

SHOPPING AND STORAGE TIPS: Choose fresh, frozen or canned corn. When selecting fresh, look for ears with green husks, shiny silks and tight rows of kernels. Refrigerate fresh corn in its husk for up to 2 days.

RECIPE

- Barbecue-Style Chicken Salad (page 141)

8 · CUCUMBER

CUCUMBER FACT: Cucumbers belong to the gourd family, which also includes squash and melons.

NUTRITION LOWDOWN: One $8\frac{1}{4}$-inch (21 cm) cucumber provides 45.15 calories, 1.96 grams of protein, 0.33 grams of fat, 10.93 grams of carbohydrates and 1.5 grams of fiber.

SHOPPING AND STORAGE TIPS: Choose fresh cucumbers that are firm and green. They should feel heavy for their size. Avoid those that are mushy, shriveled, bruised, discolored or without an intact skin. Store fresh cucumbers in a plastic bag (reusable if possible) in the refrigerator for up to 1 week.

SELECT RECIPES

- Green Smoothie with Apple and Celery (page 45)
- Mojito Smoothie (page 46)
- Green Power Drink (page 53)
- Tuna-Filled Cucumber Boats (page 56)
- Tomato Cucumber Gazpacho (page 80)
- Pita with Eggplant, Egg and Tahini (page 100)
- Smoked Salmon and Vegetable Sliders (page 109)
- Easy Cucumber Salad (page 115)
- Chickpea Salad with Couscous (page 124)
- Greek Salad with Edamame (page 125)
- Lentil Salad with Chopped Vegetables (page 127)
- Panzanella Salad with Mozzarella and Grouper (page 137)
- Easy Rotisserie Chicken Salad (page 142)

9 · LETTUCE

LETTUCE FACT: The darker the lettuce, the more nutrients it contains.

NUTRITION LOWDOWN: One cup (250 mL) of shredded romaine lettuce provides 7.99 calories, 0.58 grams of protein, 0.14 grams of fat, 1.55 grams of carbohydrates and 0.99 gram of fiber. This variety of lettuce is high in vitamin A and a good source of folate.

SHOPPING AND STORAGE TIPS: Choose fresh lettuce heads that are closely bunched, with leaves that appear fresh. Avoid those with brown, wilted edges. Rinse and dry lettuce thoroughly with paper towels. Store in the refrigerator in a plastic bag (reusable if possible) for up to 1 week.

SELECT RECIPES

- Roasted Tomato and Turkey Sandwich (page 103)
- Veggie Chicken Salad Sandwich (page 105)
- Bell Pepper Sandwich with Tuna (page 106)
- All Greens Salad with Lemon Vinaigrette (page 122)
- Greek Salad with Edamame (page 125)
- Roasted Tomato and Shrimp Salad (page 132)
- Caesar Salad with Grilled Cod (page 134)
- BLT Salad with Chicken (page 135)
- Panzanella Salad with Mozzarella and Grouper (page 137)
- Barbecue-Style Chicken Salad (page 141)

10 · MUSHROOMS

MUSHROOM FACT: Mushrooms are commonly mistaken for a vegetable, but they're really a fungus. Nutritionally, however, they are categorized as a veggie.

NUTRITION LOWDOWN: One cup (250 mL) of sliced button mushrooms provides 15.4 calories, 2.16 grams of protein, 0.24 grams of fat, 2.28 grams of carbohydrates and 0.7 grams of fiber. Mushrooms contain a powerful antioxidant called L-ergothioneine, which has been linked to kidney and liver protection.

SHOPPING AND STORAGE TIPS: Opt for fresh, frozen, canned or dried mushrooms. Choose fresh mushrooms that are firm and evenly colored. Avoid those that are slimy or damaged or have soft spots. If all the gills are showing, the mushroom is no longer fresh. Store unwashed mushrooms in their original container or in a paper bag in the refrigerator for up to 1 week.

RECIPES
- Mushroom Bruschetta (page 67)
- Udon Noodle and Shrimp Soup (page 89)
- Mushroom Cheesesteak Sandwich (page 102)
- Roasted Salmon Bowls with Mixed Vegetables (page 161)
- Farro and Mushroom Bowls with Flounder (page 164)
- Unstuffed Pepper Bowls (page 176)

11 · ONIONS

ONION FACT: Get rid of onion breath by chewing on fresh parsley.

NUTRITION LOWDOWN: One medium yellow onion provides 54.3 calories, 1.19 grams of protein, 0.07 grams of fat, 12.3 grams of carbohydrates and 3.88 grams of fiber. Onions are high in vitamin C.

SHOPPING AND STORAGE TIPS: Choose fresh or frozen onions. When selecting fresh, look for onions that are firm, with dry, bright, smooth outer skins. Avoid those with cuts, bruises or green spots. Store whole onions at room temperature for up to 4 weeks in a cool, dry place that is well ventilated. Avoid placing them near pears, apples, celery or potatoes, since onions accelerate the ripening process of those fruits and vegetables. Sliced onions should be stored in a covered container in the refrigerator for up to 3 days.

SELECT RECIPES
- Tomato Soup with Parmesan Croutons (page 76)
- Spaghetti and Meatball Soup (page 90)
- Split Pea Soup with Ham and Barley (page 93)
- Bell Pepper Sandwich with Tuna (page 106)
- Lentil Salad with Chopped Vegetables (page 127)
- Kale and Sweet Potato Salad with Shredded Chicken (page 138)
- Warming Sweet Potato and Ricotta Bowls (page 155)
- Roasted Salmon Bowls with Mixed Vegetables (page 161)
- Fish Taco Bowls (page 162)
- Farro and Mushroom Bowls with Flounder (page 164)
- Caramelized Onions (page 191)

12 · POTATOES

POTATO FACT: The skin of a potato contains about half its total fiber, so leave on those skins when you can! Most of the other nutrients, including potassium and vitamin C, are found in the flesh.

NUTRITION LOWDOWN: One medium potato with the skin on provides 110 calories, 3 grams of protein, 0 grams of fat, 26 grams of carbohydrates and 2 grams of fiber. Potatoes are an excellent source of vitamin C and a good source of potassium and vitamin B_6.

SHOPPING AND STORAGE TIPS: Choose fresh, frozen or canned potatoes. When selecting fresh, look for potatoes that are smooth, clean and firm, without cuts, bruises or discoloration. Store them at room temperature in a cool, well-ventilated location. Do not refrigerate potatoes or leave them in sunlight, and don't wash them before storing. The best storage containers are paper or perforated plastic bags (reusable if possible).

RECIPES
- Twice-Baked Potatoes with the Works (page 64)
- Chicken, Rice and Root Vegetable Soup (page 81)
- Tuna Niçoise Salad (page 148)

13 · SPINACH

SPINACH FACT: To absorb the iron in spinach, enjoy it with foods high in vitamin C, such as lemon, orange juice or bell peppers.

NUTRITION LOWDOWN: One cup (250 mL) of fresh spinach provides 6.9 calories, 0.86 grams of protein, 0.12 grams of fat, 1.09 grams of carbohydrates and 0.66 grams of fiber. Spinach is an excellent source of vitamins A, C and K and a good source of iron, potassium, riboflavin (vitamin B_2), vitamin B_6, magnesium and copper.

SHOPPING AND STORAGE TIPS: Look for fresh, frozen or canned spinach. When choosing fresh, select crisp green bunches with no discoloration, wilting or insect damage. Store spinach in the refrigerator, loosely wrapped in a damp paper towel and then placed in a plastic bag (reusable if possible). Use within 5 days.

RECIPES
- Peach Spinach Smoothie (page 50)
- Spinach Cheddar Muffins (page 60)
- Speedy Vegetable Soup (page 85)
- Soba Noodle Salad with Vegetables and Grilled Tofu (page 128)
- Lemon Orzo Salad with Peas and Salmon (page 131)
- Easy Rotisserie Chicken Salad (page 142)
- Tuna Niçoise Salad (page 148)
- Warming Sweet Potato and Ricotta Bowls (page 155)
- Roasted Salmon Bowls with Mixed Vegetables (page 161)
- Farro and Mushroom Bowls with Flounder (page 164)

14 · SWEET POTATOES

SWEET POTATO FACT: Sweet potatoes and yams are actually two different veggies. Sweet potatoes are, strange as it might seem, sweeter and less starchy.

NUTRITION LOWDOWN: One medium baked sweet potato (skin on) provides 102.6 calories, 2.29 grams of protein, 0.17 grams of fat, 23.61 grams of carbohydrates and 3.76 grams of fiber. Sweet potatoes are high in vitamins A and C and a good source of potassium.

SHOPPING AND STORAGE TIPS: Look for fresh, frozen or canned sweet potatoes. When choosing fresh, look for firm sweet potatoes with a smooth skin; avoid those with blemishes, cracks or soft spots. Store in a cool, dark, dry place for up to 5 weeks.

RECIPES

- Kale and Sweet Potato Salad with Shredded Chicken (page 138)
- Warming Sweet Potato and Ricotta Bowls (page 155)
- Curried Chicken Bowls with Sweet Potato and Red Pepper (page 175)
- Jerk-Seasoned Pork Bowls with Sweet Potato and Pineapple (page 180)

15 · TOMATOES

TOMATO FACT: Tomatoes are actually a fruit, since they grow on a vine. Nutritionally, however, they are categorized as a veggie.

NUTRITION LOWDOWN: One fresh medium tomato provides 22.14 calories, 1.08 grams of protein, 0.25 grams of fat, 4.79 grams of carbohydrates and 1.48 grams of fiber. Tomatoes are high in vitamin C. Cooked tomatoes, including those that have been canned or processed, are higher in the antioxidant lycopene compared to fresh. Lycopene has been shown to help lower the risks of cardiovascular disease, prostate cancer and macular degeneration.

SHOPPING AND STORAGE TIPS: Choose fresh or canned tomatoes. When selecting fresh, select ones that have bright, shiny skin and firm flesh and are heavy for their size. Store fresh tomatoes at room temperature in a cool, dark place out of direct sunlight. Use within 1 week.

SELECT RECIPES

- Tuna-Filled Cucumber Boats (page 56)
- Eggplant Caponata (page 72)
- Tomato Cucumber Gazpacho (page 80)
- Speedy Vegetable Soup (page 85)
- Spaghetti and Meatball Soup (page 90)
- Pita with Eggplant, Egg and Tahini (page 100)
- Roasted Tomato and Turkey Sandwich (page 103)
- Smoked Salmon and Vegetable Sliders (page 109)
- Lemon Orzo Salad with Peas and Salmon (page 131)
- Roasted Tomato and Shrimp Salad (page 132)
- Barbecue-Style Chicken Salad (page 141)
- Cheeseburger Salad (page 143)
- Tuna Niçoise Salad (page 148)
- Tomato and White Bean Quinoa Bowls (page 156)
- Pico de Gallo (page 188)

ARE YOU EATING ENOUGH VEGETABLES?

This quiz can help you assess whether you are eating enough veggies daily or if you need to up your veggies a little or a lot. For each question, choose the response that best reflects your eating habits.

1 **I include at least 1 cup (250 mL) of leafy green vegetables (such as lettuce) or $\frac{1}{2}$ cup (125 mL) sliced or cooked vegetables (such as carrots, broccoli or green beans) at lunch**
A almost never (0 to 1 time per week)
B sometimes (2 to 3 times per week)
C almost daily (4 or more times per week)

2 **I include at least 1 cup (250 mL) of leafy green vegetables or $\frac{1}{2}$ cup (125 mL) sliced or cooked vegetables at dinner**
A almost never (0 to 1 time per week)
B sometimes (2 to 3 times per week)
C almost daily (4 or more times per week)

3 **I include at least $\frac{1}{2}$ cup (125 mL) sliced raw or cooked vegetables (such as cucumbers, carrots, celery or bell peppers) in my daily snacks**
A almost never (0 to 1 time per week)
B sometimes (2 to 3 times per week)
C almost daily (4 or more times per week)

4 **I eat a salad made with vegetables every day**
A almost never (0 to 1 time per week)
B sometimes (2 to 3 times per week)
C almost daily (4 or more times per week)

5 **I include canned and frozen vegetables in my meals and snacks**
A almost never (0 to 1 time per week)
B sometimes (2 to 3 times per week)
C almost daily (4 or more times per week)

6 **I consume 100% vegetable juice every day**
A almost never (0 to 1 time per week)
B sometimes (2 to 3 times per week)
C almost daily (4 or more times per week)

7 I juice vegetables or add them to smoothies
A never
B sometimes (1 to 2 times per week)
C almost daily (3 or more times per week)

8 I eat red and orange vegetables (such as carrots or bell peppers)
A almost never (0 to 1 time per week)
B sometimes (2 to 3 times per week)
C almost daily (4 or more times per week)

9 I eat beans, peas or lentils
A never
B sometimes (1 to 2 times per week)
C almost daily (3 or more times per week)

10 I eat starchy vegetables (such as potatoes, yams, sweet potatoes or corn)
A almost never (0 to 1 time per week)
B sometimes (2 to 3 times per week)
C almost daily (4 or more times per week)

SCORING

Add up your score. For each **A** answer, add 0 points, for each **B** add 1 point and for each **C** add 2 points. Total your points and then read on to see how you are doing with your veggie consumption.

0 TO 6 POINTS: You have some work to do. Remember that canned, frozen and fresh veggies and even 100% vegetable juice count toward your daily recommended servings. Try upping your veggies every day so your health can benefit.

7 TO 13 POINTS: You're getting there but could still use a veggie boost. Check out the recipes in this book so you can start expanding your repertoire and adding more vegetables to your diet.

14 TO 20 POINTS: Give yourself a gold star! You're already taking in the recommended daily amount of veggies, which is great work. Keep it up! The recipes in this book can help add variety to your healthy diet.

A WORD ABOUT FLEXITARIAN EATING

Back in the 1970s, a huge prime rib roast would be served with maybe a few measly pieces of broccoli on the side. Obviously, that was not plant-forward, and it certainly wasn't balanced either. Dietary guidelines have changed. It is now recommended that half your plate be composed of fruits and veggies, one-quarter of starches (especially whole grains) and one-quarter of protein — which can be from plant or animal sources — along with a serving of milk or other dairy and a healthy fat.

Some days you might eat meat and some days you might not. This is called a flexitarian approach to eating, which has also been termed "semi-vegetarian." It's an omnivorous plan (inclusive of both plant and animal foods) and it emphasizes what you should put on your plate rather than foods that should be eliminated. As a registered dietitian, I enjoy both animal and plant foods and believe that they can complement each other, both taste-wise and nutritionally.

By definition, eating flexitarian means being flexible. On different days of the week, you may decide that your protein will be 5 oz (150 g) of grilled salmon, $\frac{1}{2}$ cup (125 mL) of canned beans or 3 oz (90 g) of cooked beef tenderloin. This cookbook will enable you to try a variety of recipes while also giving you the flexibility to swap proteins if you choose. The most important part of this approach is to make sure you're getting your veggies and reaping the benefits of this important group of foods!

CHAPTER 2

MAKING COOKING EASY

This cookbook is intended to help you eat more vegetables while also streamlining your time in the kitchen. My recipes use popular ingredients that are easy to find at your local supermarket, but please keep in mind that I want you to feel comfortable about upping your vegetables in whichever way works for you. You'll find information in the following pages to help you stay organized in the kitchen, even in the busiest of weeks. Meal-prepping and freezing dishes can help ensure that you have food ready to eat whenever you're in a time crunch.

MEAL-PREPPING

Meal-prepping involves preparing meals on one day to eat throughout the week. If you choose to do this, I recommend following these five steps:

STEP 1

CHOOSE WHEN TO PREP. You don't always have to prep your meals over a weekend. If you have a job where you're off during the week or want to split your prep day in two, do whatever works best for your schedule.

STEP 2

DECIDE WHICH MEALS TO PREP. You don't have to prep every single meal for the whole week. You can opt to make dinners only, or lunch and dinner, or even snacks. Just don't overwhelm yourself. Prepping even two or three recipes will help you save time during a busy work week. Look for the meal-prep icon (see page 34) throughout the book to find recipes that are easy to make in advance.

STEP 3

GO FOOD SHOPPING. Using the recipes you've selected for the week, make a shopping list. Check to see if you already have the spices and other ingredients that are required. The last thing you need is a third jar of onion powder! When making your list, group foods the way they are organized in the store: fruits, veggies, frozen, meat/chicken/fish, milk and dairy, and pantry items. This will help you be faster at the supermarket. Give yourself an appropriate amount of time to get to the store, do your shopping, get home and unpack your groceries.

STEP 4

PREP AND COOK. Start by marinating your proteins and getting your veggies ready. Next, prepare the recipes that take longer to cook. You can make dressings and less time-consuming dishes while the longer recipes are cooking. It takes a little practice to get into the swing of things, which is why I recommend starting with fewer recipes and building your way up.

STEP 5

PORTION AND PACK. This is the most important step in meal-prepping, and one that is often forgotten. If you don't portion and package your food, you can end up serving too much in your initial meals, leaving you with less than a full portion at the end. This step also ensures that you're getting the nutrition listed in the recipe information.

Choose containers that fit your lifestyle, storage space and budget. Knowing how long the food will last is also an important part of this step. As a general rule, heat-and-eat bowls can be stored in the refrigerator for up to four days. Any leftovers can go in the freezer for up to two months in a freezer-friendly container. Much depends on the ingredients — salads and sandwiches can get soggy and may not last more than two or three days. If either of these items is part of your meal plan, you may want to split your prep days, with one a few days after the first, to maximize freshness.

FREEZER-FRIENDLY MEALS

The recipes appropriate for freezing have an icon that makes it easy for you to identify them. Typically, soups and bowls are freezer friendly. Once you've cooked your recipe, allow the food to cool to room temperature (about 70°F/21°C) and then transfer it to individual or family-size freezer-friendly containers. Do not allow leftovers to sit on the counter for more than two hours. Cover the containers, label with the recipe name and date, and store in the freezer for up to two months.

To defrost, place the container in the refrigerator one to two nights before you wish to eat it. Reheat in the microwave (in a microwave-safe dish), on the stovetop or in the oven.

ONE-POT MEALS

Save time (and cleanup!) in the kitchen by making smoothies and one-pot or sheet-pan meals. In this cookbook, soups and smoothies tend to be the most common recipes that use only one pot or piece of equipment.

30 MINUTES OR LESS

When you can complete a recipe from start to finish in 30 minutes or less, it's a total win! One shortcut to help get a meal on the table quickly is using canned and frozen foods. In this cookbook, I use a ton of canned beans, canned lentils and canned tomatoes. Taking such shortcuts can help shave off minutes and even hours in the kitchen.

ICON GUIDES

Each recipe in this book was reviewed and given a symbol if it met the criteria for any of the following labels:

MEAL PREP
The recipe can be prepared in advance.

FREEZER-FRIENDLY
The recipe is appropriate for freezing.

ONE POT/PAN MEAL
The recipe can be prepared in a blender or cooked with just one pot or pan (which means fewer dishes!).

30 MINUTES OR LESS
The recipe can be prepared and cooked in half an hour or less.

VEGETARIAN
The recipe contains only plant foods, milk and/or other dairy products, and/or eggs.

VEGAN
The recipe contains no animal products, including honey.

DAIRY-FREE
The recipe contains no milk or other dairy products. Note that some packaged ingredients may be prepared in a facility that uses dairy products, so make sure to read the nutrition facts and ingredients panels carefully.

GLUTEN-FREE
The recipe has no ingredients that contain gluten. Note that some packaged ingredients may be prepared in a facility where they come in contact with gluten, so make sure to read the nutrition facts and ingredients panels carefully.

In Chapters 9 and 10 (pages 185 to 199), the icons have be reduced in size and do not contain an image. Each colored box corresponds to the color of the larger icon.

In addition to the icons, you'll also find a Toby's Tip in most recipes. My tips provide guidance for making substitutions or swaps, using leftover ingredients and adding even more veggies to your dish. You can never have too many vegetables!

A WORD ON NUTRITION INFORMATION

Every recipe in this cookbook contains nutrition information for one serving. You will find information on calories; grams of total fat, saturated fat, protein, total carbohydrates, fiber and total sugars; and milligrams of sodium and cholesterol. This information is provided for your convenience or if you require guidance about specific nutrients.

CHAPTER 3

SMOOTHIES

CAULIFLOWER-BERRY SMOOTHIE

Cauliflower is a great addition to your morning or snack-time smoothie. Not only does the cruciferous veggie help decrease the risk of certain forms of cancer, but ricing and freezing it also gives your smoothie an icy texture.

SERVES 2 | SERVING SIZE: 1 CUP (250 ML)

Blender

1 cup (250 mL) frozen riced cauliflower

1 cup (250 mL) frozen raspberries

1 cup (250 mL) frozen strawberries

¾ cup (175 mL) vanilla nonfat Greek yogurt

½ cup (125 mL) 100% pomegranate juice or cranberry juice

1　In a blender, combine the cauliflower, raspberries, strawberries, Greek yogurt and pomegranate juice; blend on high speed until smooth, about 1 minute.

2　Divide evenly between two glasses and serve immediately.

Toby's Tip

You can find riced cauliflower in the produce section of your supermarket or in the freezer aisle alongside the frozen vegetables.

NUTRITION INFORMATION (PER SERVING)	Calories: 180 • Total Fat: 0 g • Saturated Fat: 0 g
	Protein: 10 g • Total Carbohydrates: 36 g • Fiber: 6 g
	Sugars: 25 g • Sodium: 55 mg • Cholesterol: 0 mg

ZUCCHINI BREAD SMOOTHIE

Enjoy the flavor of your favorite zucchini bread in a glass, but with fewer calories! I like to keep the skin on the zucchini for some extra fiber.

SERVES 2 | SERVING SIZE: 1¼ CUPS (310 ML)

Blender

1 cup (250 mL) nonfat milk

¼ cup (60 mL) large-flake (old-fashioned) rolled oats

½ cup (125 mL) ice cubes

1 medium zucchini, roughly chopped

1 medium banana, halved

¼ cup (60 mL) raw walnuts, chopped

2 tsp (10 mL) pure maple syrup

½ tsp (2 mL) ground cinnamon

⅛ tsp (0.5 mL) ground nutmeg

1   In a blender, stir together the milk and oats. Let stand for at least 10 minutes or up to 30 minutes.

2   Add the ice cubes, zucchini, banana, walnuts, maple syrup, cinnamon and nutmeg to the blender; blend on high speed until smooth, about 1 minute.

3   Divide evenly between two glasses and serve immediately.

Toby's Tip

Swap the nonfat milk for soy or another plant-based beverage to make this smoothie vegan and dairy-free.

NUTRITION INFORMATION (PER SERVING)

Calories: 211 • Total Fat: 4 g • Saturated Fat: 1 g
Protein: 8 g • Total Carbohydrates: 40 g • Fiber: 5 g
Sugars: 24 g • Sodium: 60 mg • Cholesterol: 2 mg

SUNSHINE SMOOTHIE

Wake up to this gorgeous orange-hued smoothie bursting with flavor and nutrition. Between the carrots, pineapple, orange and lemon juices, and banana, you'll be taking in a healthy dose of beta-carotene, vitamin C, potassium and fiber.

SERVES 2 | SERVING SIZE: 1 CUP (250 ML)

Blender

4 carrots, roughly chopped

1 cup (250 mL) frozen pineapple chunks

1 medium banana, halved

1 cup (250 mL) 100% orange juice

1 tbsp (15 mL) freshly squeezed lemon juice

1 tbsp (15 mL) honey

⅛ tsp (0.5 mL) ground ginger

1 In a blender, combine the carrots, pineapple, banana, orange juice, lemon juice, honey and ginger; blend on high until smooth, about 1 minute.

2 Divide evenly between two glasses and serve immediately.

Toby's Tip

If you like your smoothie with an icier texture, slice and freeze the carrots before using.

NUTRITION INFORMATION (PER SERVING)	Calories: 291 • Total Fat: 1 g • Saturated Fat: 0 g
	Protein: 4 g • Total Carbohydrates: 71 g • Fiber: 9 g
	Sugars: 50 g • Sodium: 113 mg • Cholesterol: 0 mg

TROPICAL GREEN SMOOTHIE

The base of this green smoothie is spinach, which provides vitamins A, C and K, as well as iron, folate and fiber. You get even more antioxidant vitamins and phytonutrients by pairing it with mango and pineapple.

SERVES 2 | SERVING SIZE: 1½ CUPS (375 ML)

Blender

1 cup (250 mL) lightly packed baby spinach

¾ cup (175 mL) frozen mango chunks

¾ cup (175 mL) frozen pineapple chunks

1 medium banana, halved

1 cup (250 mL) unsweetened light coconut milk

1   In a blender, combine the spinach, mango, pineapple, banana and coconut milk; blend on high speed until smooth, about 1 minute.

2   Divide evenly between two glasses and serve immediately.

Toby's Tip

Swap the spinach for chopped kale.

NUTRITION INFORMATION (PER SERVING)	Calories: 211 • Total Fat: 6 g • Saturated Fat: 6 g
	Protein: 3 g • Total Carbohydrates: 40 g • Fiber: 5 g
	Sugars: 26 g • Sodium: 51 mg • Cholesterol: 0 mg

PURPLE SMOOTHIE

This refreshingly healthy and flavorful smoothie has a ton of antioxidants. I like to add Greek yogurt for some protein and creaminess, which makes it a well-balanced snack you can enjoy any time of day.

SERVES 2 | SERVING SIZE: 1¼ CUPS (310 ML)

Blender

1 cup (250 mL) frozen wild blueberries (see Toby's Tip)

1 cup (250 mL) shredded red cabbage

1 small banana, halved

¾ cup (175 mL) vanilla nonfat Greek yogurt

¾ cup (175 mL) 100% pomegranate juice or cranberry juice

1   In a blender, combine the blueberries, cabbage, banana, Greek yogurt and pomegranate juice; blend on high speed until smooth, about 1 minute.

2   Divide evenly between two glasses and serve immediately.

Toby's Tip

Wild blueberries are sweeter and slightly smaller than regular blueberries and can be found in the freezer section of the supermarket. You can always use fresh or frozen regular blueberries instead of the wild variety.

NUTRITION INFORMATION (PER SERVING)

Calories: 173 • Total Fat: 0 g • Saturated Fat: 0 g

Protein: 10 g • Total Carbohydrates: 34 g • Fiber: 5 g

Sugars: 16 g • Sodium: 47 mg • Cholesterol: 0 mg

GREEN SMOOTHIE
WITH APPLE AND CELERY

The tart flavor of a Granny Smith apple blends beautifully with celery, cucumber and sweet apple juice. All these fruits and veggies also add nutrition to your day, including vitamins C and K.

SERVES 2 | SERVING SIZE: 1 CUP (250 ML)

Blender

1 medium Granny Smith apple, roughly chopped

1 celery stalk, roughly chopped

½ English cucumber, roughly chopped

¾ cup (175 mL) 100% apple juice

⅛ tsp (0.5 mL) ground ginger

1　In a blender, combine the apple, celery, cucumber, apple juice and ginger; blend on high speed until smooth, about 1 minute.

2　Divide evenly between two glasses and serve immediately.

Toby's Tip

Leave the skin on your fruits and veggies (including the apple and cucumber in this smoothie). Skin adds more fiber.

NUTRITION INFORMATION (PER SERVING)

Calories: 108 • Total Fat: 0 g • Saturated Fat: 0 g
Protein: 1 g • Total Carbohydrates: 24 g • Fiber: 4 g
Sugars: 18 g • Sodium: 21 mg • Cholesterol: 0 mg

MOJITO SMOOTHIE

Cucumbers have a mild flavor and are full of water (96 percent!), making them an easy addition to smoothies. Combine them with mint, lime juice and a touch of agave (sans the alcohol) and you can enjoy that mojito flavor any time of day.

SERVES 2 | SERVING SIZE: 1 CUP (250 ML)

Blender

1 cup (250 mL) frozen pineapple chunks

½ English cucumber, roughly chopped

¾ cup (175 mL) 100% apple juice

1 tbsp (15 mL) freshly squeezed lime juice

2 tsp (10 mL) agave nectar or honey

4 mint leaves

1   In a blender, combine the pineapple, cucumber, apple juice, lime juice, agave nectar and mint; blend on high speed until smooth, about 1 minute.

2   Divide evenly between two glasses and serve immediately.

Toby's Tip

To store fresh mint leaves, place between moist paper towels in an unsealed plastic bag. Keep in the refrigerator for up to 3 days.

NUTRITION INFORMATION (PER SERVING)

Calories: 272 • Total Fat: 0 g • Saturated Fat: 0 g

Protein: 3 g • Total Carbohydrates: 65 g • Fiber: 7 g

Sugars: 55 g • Sodium: 8 mg • Cholesterol: 0 mg

RUBY RED SMOOTHIE

Red bell pepper in a smoothie? Absolutely! You only need half a red pepper to add a nice punch to this drink. Plus, one cup (250 mL) chopped red bell pepper contains three times more vitamin C than an orange!

SERVES 2 | SERVING SIZE: 1 CUP (250 ML)

Blender

¾ cup (175 mL) frozen raspberries

¾ cup (175 mL) frozen strawberries

½ red bell pepper, seeded and quartered

¼ English cucumber, roughly chopped

¾ cup (175 mL) 100% pomegranate juice or cranberry juice

1 In a blender, combine the raspberries, strawberries, bell pepper, cucumber and pomegranate juice; blend on high speed until smooth, about 1 minute.

2 Divide evenly between two glasses and serve immediately.

Toby's Tip

Look for 100% juice, which provides various phytonutrients. These nutrients, found naturally in food, help keep you healthy and may also aid in preventing disease.

NUTRITION INFORMATION (PER SERVING)

Calories: 123 • Total Fat: 1 g • Saturated Fat: 0 g
Protein: 2 g • Total Carbohydrates: 30 g • Fiber: 6 g
Sugars: 21 g • Sodium: 12 mg • Cholesterol: 0 mg

PEACH SPINACH SMOOTHIE

Spinach blends nicely with a variety of flavors. In this smoothie, the sweet tastes of peach and mandarin orange balance the light, mild flavor of the spinach.

SERVES 2 | SERVING SIZE: 1¼ CUPS (310 ML)

Blender

1 cup (250 mL) frozen peach slices

1 cup (250 mL) lightly packed baby spinach

¾ cup (175 mL) vanilla nonfat Greek yogurt

½ cup (125 mL) nonfat milk

½ cup (125 mL) mandarin orange fruit cup or canned mandarin oranges in 100% juice or water

2 tsp (10 mL) honey

1 In a blender, combine the peach slices, spinach, Greek yogurt, milk, mandarin orange pieces (with liquid) and honey; blend on high speed until smooth, about 1 minute.

2 Divide evenly between two glasses and serve immediately.

Toby's Tip

Canned fruit can be a healthy option, but be mindful about added sugar. It's best to choose those that are packed in water or their own juice whenever possible. The next best option is canned fruit packed in extra-light or light syrup.

NUTRITION INFORMATION (PER SERVING)	Calories: 153 • Total Fat: 0 g • Saturated Fat: 0 g Protein: 11 g • Total Carbohydrates: 28 g • Fiber: 2 g Sugars: 25 g • Sodium: 84 mg • Cholesterol: 1 mg

PUMPKIN PIE SMOOTHIE

This smoothie captures the flavors of fall in one refreshing glass. Use pumpkin purée and not canned pumpkin pie filling, which is packed with added sugar.

SERVES 2 | SERVING SIZE: 1 CUP (250 ML)

Blender

1 medium banana, halved

¾ cup (175 mL) canned pumpkin purée

¾ cup (175 mL) vanilla nonfat Greek yogurt

¾ cup (175 mL) nonfat milk

2 tbsp (30 mL) raw walnuts, roughly chopped

¾ tsp (3 mL) pumpkin pie spice

1 In a blender, combine the banana, pumpkin purée, Greek yogurt, milk, walnuts and pumpkin pie spice; blend on high speed until smooth, about 1 minute.

2 Divide evenly between two glasses and serve immediately.

Toby's Tip

If you want to give your smoothie a little more kick, add an additional ¼ tsp (1 mL) pumpkin pie spice.

NUTRITION INFORMATION (PER SERVING)	Calories: 197 • Total Fat: 2 g • Saturated Fat: 0 g
	Protein: 14 g • Total Carbohydrates: 34 g • Fiber: 5 g
	Sugars: 22 g • Sodium: 78 mg • Cholesterol: 2 mg

CHERRY, ALMOND AND KALE SMOOTHIE

Kale is a green leafy vegetable brimming with vitamins and minerals. For this smoothie, I like to combine it with cherries for sweetness and nut butter to give you some healthy fat and protein.

SERVES 2 | SERVING SIZE: 1¼ CUPS (310 ML)

Blender

1½ cups (375 mL) pitted frozen cherries

1 cup (250 mL) roughly chopped curly kale (see Toby's Tip)

2 pitted dates

¾ cup (175 mL) vanilla nonfat Greek yogurt

¾ cup (175 mL) unsweetened almond milk or nonfat milk

2 tbsp (30 mL) almond butter

1 In a blender, combine the cherries, kale, dates, Greek yogurt, almond milk and almond butter; blend on high speed until smooth, about 1 minute.

2 Divide evenly between two glasses and serve immediately.

Toby's Tip

Remove any thick stems from the kale before using.

NUTRITION INFORMATION (PER SERVING)	Calories: 325 • Total Fat: 10 g • Saturated Fat: 1 g
	Protein: 15 g • Total Carbohydrates: 48 g • Fiber: 7 g
	Sugars: 37 g • Sodium: 114 mg • Cholesterol: 0 mg

GREEN POWER DRINK

This power drink is the perfect post-exercise snack because it gives you a great combination of protein and carbs, both of which you need after you work out!

SERVES 2 | SERVING SIZE: 1⅓ CUPS (325 ML)

Blender

½ cup (125 mL) frozen peas, thawed

¼ cup (60 mL) water

2 cups (500 mL) chopped seedless watermelon

½ English cucumber, roughly chopped

1 cup (250 mL) ice cubes

¼ cup (60 mL) 100% apple juice

2 tsp (10 mL) honey or agave nectar

4 mint leaves

1 In a small saucepan, combine the peas and water; bring to a boil over high heat. Reduce the heat to low and simmer until heated through, about 5 minutes. Remove the saucepan from the heat and let cool for 10 minutes. Drain and set aside.

2 In a blender, combine the cooled peas, watermelon, cucumber, ice cubes, apple juice, honey and mint; blend on high speed until smooth, about 1 minute.

3 Divide evenly between two glasses and serve immediately.

Toby's Tip

Choose frozen peas or no-salt-added canned peas for this smoothie. Too much salt will throw off the flavor.

NUTRITION INFORMATION (PER SERVING)

Calories: 117 • Total Fat: 0 g • Saturated Fat: 0 g
Protein: 4 g • Total Carbohydrates: 27 g • Fiber: 3 g
Sugars: 21 g • Sodium: 44 mg • Cholesterol: 0 mg

CHAPTER 4

SNACKS AND APPETIZERS

TUNA-FILLED CUCUMBER BOATS

When you combine various food groups you get way more health benefits from the dish. The protein from the tuna and fiber from the cucumber help keep you feeling fuller longer. This is perfect to get you from one meal to the next or to enjoy as your evening snack.

SERVES 3 | SERVING SIZE: 2 PIECES

3 medium cucumbers, ends trimmed and sliced lengthwise

3 tbsp (45 mL) light mayonnaise

3 tbsp (45 mL) plain nonfat Greek yogurt

2 tsp (10 mL) Dijon mustard

1 tsp (5 mL) freshly squeezed lemon juice

2 tsp (10 mL) chopped fresh parsley

¼ tsp (1 mL) salt

⅛ tsp (0.5 mL) ground black pepper

2 cans (each 5 oz/75 g) water-packed chunk light tuna, drained

½ medium red onion, finely chopped

1 celery stalk, finely chopped

6 cherry tomatoes, halved lengthwise

1 Using a spoon, scrape the seeds out of the cucumbers, leaving a 1-inch (2.5 cm) canal. Cut the cucumbers in half and place on a plate or cutting board.

2 In a medium bowl, combine the mayonnaise, Greek yogurt, mustard, lemon juice, parsley, salt and pepper. Add the tuna, onion and celery; stir to combine.

3 Spread the tuna mixture evenly in the canal of each cucumber piece. Top each with 1 tomato half. Serve immediately or store in an airtight container in the refrigerator for up to 4 days.

Toby's Tip

To minimize food waste, use the leftover cucumber flesh in a smoothie.

NUTRITION INFORMATION (PER SERVING)	Calories: 105 • Total Fat: 2 g • Saturated Fat: 0 g
	Protein: 13 g • Total Carbohydrates: 9 g • Fiber: 1 g
	Sugars: 4 g • Sodium: 421 mg • Cholesterol: 27 mg

GREEK SALAD SKEWERS

Food always tastes better on skewers! Enjoy these as a snack, dipped in your favorite dressing (see Toby's Tip). You can also serve them as an appetizer at a dinner party or pack them as part of a lunch. If you choose to prepare this recipe in advance, store the skewers in an airtight container in the refrigerator for up to 4 days.

SERVES 4 | SERVING SIZE: 3 SKEWERS

Twelve 4-inch (10 cm) skewers

1 green bell pepper, cut into twelve 1-inch (2.5 cm) pieces

3½ oz (110 g) feta cheese, cut into twelve 1-inch (2.5 cm) cubes

12 grape tomatoes

12 pitted kalamata olives

¼ English cucumber, sliced lengthwise and cut into twelve 1-inch (2.5 cm) slices

1 Thread each skewer with one piece each of the bell pepper, feta cheese, tomato, olive and cucumber.

2 Place the skewers on a large platter; serve.

Toby's Tip

Serve with Balsamic Vinaigrette (page 194) for dipping.

NUTRITION INFORMATION (PER SERVING)	Calories: 104 • Total Fat: 7 g • Saturated Fat: 4 g Protein: 5 g • Total Carbohydrates: 5 g • Fiber: 1 g Sugars: 3 g • Sodium: 429 mg • Cholesterol: 22 mg

SPINACH CHEDDAR MUFFINS

These savory muffins are a great on-the-go snack, or you can make them in mini muffin pans and serve them to guests as an appetizer (see Toby's Tip). Whichever size you choose, they're a delicious way to get in some of your daily veggies.

SERVES 12 | SERVING SIZE: 1 MUFFIN

12-cup muffin pan coated with nonstick cooking spray

2 tbsp (30 mL) olive oil	½ tsp (2 mL) onion powder
4 cups (1 L) lightly packed baby spinach	½ tsp (2 mL) salt
1 cup (250 mL) unbleached all-purpose flour	2 large eggs
½ cup (125 mL) 100% whole wheat flour	½ cup (125 mL) low-fat milk
1½ tsp (7 mL) baking powder	¼ cup (60 mL) plain reduced-fat Greek yogurt
1 tsp (5 mL) dried oregano	¼ cup (60 mL) unsalted butter, melted
1 tsp (5 mL) dried parsley	1¼ cups (310 mL) shredded reduced-fat sharp (old) Cheddar cheese
½ tsp (2 mL) garlic powder	

PREHEAT THE OVEN TO 350°F (180°C).

1 In a large skillet, heat the olive oil over medium heat until shimmering. Add the spinach; cook, stirring occasionally, until wilted, about 4 minutes. Remove from the heat and let cool slightly.

2 In a medium bowl, whisk together the all-purpose flour, whole wheat flour, baking powder, oregano, parsley, garlic powder, onion powder and salt.

3 In a large bowl, whisk together the eggs, milk, Greek yogurt and melted butter. Add the Cheddar cheese; stir to combine. Add the flour mixture; stir until just combined (do not overmix). Gently fold in the cooked spinach.

4 Spoon the batter into the prepared muffin cups until three-quarters full. Gently tap the pan a few times to remove any air bubbles.

5 Bake on the center rack of the preheated oven until a toothpick inserted in the center of a muffin comes out clean, 18 to 20 minutes.

6 Remove from the oven and let cool in the pan for 10 minutes, then transfer to a wire rack to cool for 10 minutes more. Enjoy immediately or store at room temperature in an airtight container for up to 4 days. Microwave for 15 seconds before eating.

NUTRITION INFORMATION (PER SERVING)	Calories: 169 • Total Fat: 9 g • Saturated Fat: 5 g
	Protein: 7 g • Total Carbohydrates: 13 g • Fiber: 1 g
	Sugars: 1 g • Sodium: 279 mg • Cholesterol: 49 mg

Toby's Tip

You can also make these in a mini muffin pan. Just reduce the cooking time to 15 to 18 minutes.

ROASTED CARROT HUMMUS

This dip has become a favorite in my house, and hopefully it will become one in yours, too! I like to serve it with vegetables, crackers or crusty bread.

SERVES 8 | SERVING SIZE: ¼ CUP (60 ML)

Rimmed baking sheet lined with parchment paper or a silicone mat

Blender

1 lb (500 g) carrots, cut into 2-inch (5 cm) slices	1 garlic clove, crushed
6 tbsp (90 mL) olive oil, divided	2 tbsp (30 mL) freshly squeezed lemon juice
¼ tsp (1 mL) salt, divided	1 tsp (5 mL) ground cumin
¼ tsp (1 mL) ground black pepper, divided	½ tsp (2 mL) smoked paprika
1¾ cups (425 mL) low-sodium canned chickpeas, drained and rinsed	½ tsp (2 mL) chili powder

PREHEAT THE OVEN TO 425°F (220°C).

1 In a medium bowl, combine the carrots, 2 tbsp (30 mL) olive oil, ⅛ tsp (0.5 mL) salt and ⅛ tsp (0.5 mL) pepper; toss to coat. Transfer the carrots to the prepared baking sheet in a single layer.

2 Bake in the preheated oven until the carrots are slightly browned, about 15 minutes. Remove from the oven and let cool slightly.

3 In a blender, combine the roasted carrots, chickpeas, garlic, lemon juice, cumin, paprika, chili powder, and remaining ⅛ tsp (0.5 mL) salt and ⅛ tsp (0.5 mL) pepper; blend on high speed until smooth. With the blender running on low speed, slowly add the remaining ¼ cup (60 mL) olive oil and pulse until smooth.

4 Transfer to a dip bowl and serve immediately, or store in an airtight container in the refrigerator for up to 4 days.

Toby's Tip

Swap the chickpeas for white beans such as great northern or cannellini.

NUTRITION INFORMATION (PER SERVING)	Calories: 152 • Total Fat: 11 g • Saturated Fat: 1 g
	Protein: 4 g • Total Carbohydrates: 14 g • Fiber: 4 g
	Sugars: 4 g • Sodium: 212 mg • Cholesterol: 0 mg

TWICE-BAKED POTATOES WITH THE WORKS

Did you know potatoes have more potassium than bananas? Not to mention that one medium potato provides 30 percent of your recommended daily vitamin C. And let's not forget the fiber and protein. Plus, adding bacon, sour cream and a touch of butter makes them unbelievably tasty!

SERVES 6 | SERVING SIZE: 1 HALF-POTATO

Rimmed baking sheet, lined with parchment paper or a silicone mat

3 russet potatoes (about 3 lbs/1.5 kg total)

Nonstick cooking spray

3 slices turkey bacon

½ cup (125 mL) shredded reduced-fat Mexican-style cheese blend

½ cup (125 mL) low-fat milk

¼ cup (60 mL) reduced-fat sour cream

2 tbsp (30 mL) unsalted butter, softened

¼ tsp (1 mL) salt

⅛ tsp (0.5 mL) ground black pepper

2 tbsp (30 mL) chives, cut into ½-inch (1 cm) pieces (optional)

PREHEAT THE OVEN TO 425°F (220°C).

1   Using a fork, poke several holes in each potato. Place on the prepared baking sheet and bake in the preheated oven until tender, about 1 hour. Remove from the oven and let cool slightly, reserving baking sheet. Do not turn off the oven.

2   Meanwhile, coat a large skillet with cooking spray. Heat over medium heat until hot. Add the turkey bacon and cook, turning occasionally, until crispy, 8 to 10 minutes. Remove the bacon from the skillet and place on a cutting board; chop finely.

3   Once the potatoes are cool enough to handle, slice them in half lengthwise. Without tearing the skin, gently scoop out the flesh and place in a medium bowl. Add the bacon pieces, Mexican cheese blend, milk, sour cream, butter, salt and pepper. Using a potato masher, mash until combined.

4   Place the potato skins back on the prepared baking sheet. Spoon the potato mixture evenly into the skins.

5   Return to the oven until warmed through, about 20 minutes. Sprinkle chives evenly overtop (if using) and serve immediately.

Toby's Tip

If you're looking to make this recipe gluten-free, check the bacon package to make sure it is gluten-free.

NUTRITION INFORMATION (PER SERVING)   Calories: 334 • Total Fat: 10 g • Saturated Fat: 5 g
Protein: 11 g • Total Carbohydrates: 50 g • Fiber: 5 g
Sugars: 5 g • Sodium: 379 mg • Cholesterol: 38 mg

MUSHROOM BRUSCHETTA

This bruschetta is a delicious finger food to serve to guests. The umami-rich mushrooms, balsamic vinegar, thyme and pomegranate juice create a flavor explosion in your mouth!

SERVES 6 | SERVING SIZE: 3 PIECES

Rimmed baking sheet lined with parchment paper or a silicone mat

¼ cup (60 mL) olive oil, divided

½ tsp (2 mL) salt, divided

1 French baguette (7 oz/210 g), whole wheat preferred, cut into eighteen ¾-inch (2 cm) slices

1 garlic clove, minced

10 oz (300 g) cremini mushrooms, thinly sliced

2 tbsp (30 mL) 100% pomegranate juice

1 tbsp (15 mL) balsamic vinegar

1 tsp (5 mL) chopped fresh thyme

⅛ tsp (0.5 mL) ground black pepper

2 tbsp (30 mL) grated Parmesan cheese

PREHEAT THE OVEN TO 400°F (200°C).

1 In a small bowl, combine 2 tbsp (30 mL) olive oil and ¼ tsp (1 mL) salt. Brush the oil mixture over both sides of the baguette slices. Place on the prepared baking sheet in a single layer.

2 Bake the bread slices in the preheated oven, turning them halfway through, until golden brown, about 10 minutes.

3 Meanwhile, in a large skillet, heat the remaining 2 tbsp (30 mL) olive oil over medium heat until shimmering. Add the garlic and cook until fragrant, about 30 seconds. Add the mushrooms; cook, stirring occasionally, until softened, about 5 minutes. Add the pomegranate juice, balsamic vinegar, thyme, the remaining ¼ tsp (1 mL) salt and pepper; increase the heat to high and bring to a boil. Reduce the heat to medium-low and simmer, stirring occasionally, until most of the liquid has evaporated, about 5 minutes. Remove the skillet from the heat and let cool slightly.

4 Place the toasted bread slices on a large serving platter. Spoon 1 tbsp (15 mL) of the mushroom mixture onto each of the slices and sprinkle each with an equal amount of Parmesan cheese. Serve immediately.

Toby's Tip

Swap the 100% pomegranate juice for 2 tsp (10 mL) honey or agave syrup.

NUTRITION INFORMATION (PER SERVING)

Calories: 192 • Total Fat: 10 g • Saturated Fat: 2 g

Protein: 6 g • Total Carbohydrates: 21 g • Fiber: 1 g

Sugars: 2 g • Sodium: 424 mg • Cholesterol: 2 mg

JALAPEÑO POPPER WONTON CUPS

This fun spin on jalapeño poppers will have your mouth dancing in delight. The crunchy wonton wrappers are filled with a creamy, spicy mixture of jalapeños, cheese and green onion. If you want a little more heat, do not remove the jalapeño seeds.

SERVES 8 | SERVING SIZE: 2 WONTON CUPS

At least 16-cup mini muffin pan coated with nonstick cooking spray

3 jalapeño peppers, seeded and finely chopped

½ cup (125 mL) whipped cream cheese

⅔ cup (150 mL) shredded reduced-fat sharp (old) Cheddar cheese, divided

2 green onions, finely chopped

¼ tsp (1 mL) salt

16 wonton wrappers

PREHEAT THE OVEN TO 350°F (180°C).

1 In a medium bowl, combine the jalapeños, cream cheese, ½ cup (125 mL) Cheddar cheese, green onions and salt.

2 Using clean hands, gently push each wonton wrapper into one of the muffin cups. Spoon the mixture evenly into the wonton wrappers. Sprinkle the remaining 2 tbsp (30 mL) Cheddar cheese evenly overtop.

3 Bake in the preheated oven, until the wonton wrappers are cooked through and the cheese topping has melted, about 10 minutes. Serve warm.

Toby's Tip

You can find wonton wrappers most often in the refrigerated section of Asian supermarkets or near the produce section in your local supermarket.

NUTRITION INFORMATION (PER SERVING)
Calories: 104 • Total Fat: 5 g • Saturated Fat: 3 g
Protein: 5 g • Total Carbohydrates: 11 g • Fiber: 1 g
Sugars: 1 g • Sodium: 275 mg • Cholesterol: 16 mg

ROASTED RED PEPPER DEVILED EGGS

This is a veggied-up twist on deviled eggs that uses savory-sweet roasted red peppers. Whether you serve them to your kids after school or to guests at a cocktail party, deviled eggs are always a big hit. I like to boil the eggs a day or two in advance to save time.

SERVES 6 | SERVING SIZE: 2 HALF-EGGS

Food processor

Medium piping bag fitted with a closed star tip (optional)

6 large eggs

4 oz (125 g) jarred roasted red peppers, drained

2 tbsp (30 mL) light mayonnaise

1 tsp (5 mL) Dijon mustard

½ tsp (2 mL) smoked paprika

¼ tsp (1 mL) garlic powder

¼ tsp (1 mL) salt

⅛ tsp (0.5 mL) cayenne pepper

1 green onion, green part only, chopped

1 Place eggs in a medium saucepan and cover with cold water; bring to a boil over high heat. Continue boiling for 3 minutes, then remove from the heat, cover and let stand for 15 minutes. Drain; run cold water over the eggs until completely cool, about 10 minutes.

2 Once the eggs are cool enough to handle, peel and cut them in half lengthwise. Remove the yolks and set 3 aside. Discard the remaining yolks or reserve for another use (see Toby's Tip). Place the egg whites on a plate, cover and refrigerate for at least 20 minutes or up to 24 hours.

3 Meanwhile, in a food processor, combine the 3 egg yolks, roasted red peppers, mayonnaise, mustard, paprika, garlic powder, salt and cayenne pepper; pulse until smooth. Transfer the mixture to a piping bag fitted with a closed star tip or a medium resealable bag with a corner cut off; refrigerate until needed.

4 Pipe an even amount of the yolks mixture into each egg half. Garnish with green onion. Serve at room temperature within 2 hours of preparation, or cover and store in the refrigerator for up to 4 days.

Toby's Tip

I like to chop the leftover cooked egg yolks and add them to salads, or I mash them to top avocado toast.

NUTRITION INFORMATION (PER SERVING)
Calories: 59 • Total Fat: 4 g • Saturated Fat: 1 g
Protein: 5 g • Total Carbohydrates: 1 g • Fiber: 0 g
Sugars: 0 g • Sodium: 223 mg • Cholesterol: 94 mg

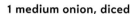

EGGPLANT CAPONATA

This Mediterranean-inspired vegetable mixture is a savory, salty combination that melts in your mouth. Enjoy it warm or cold with whole wheat pita or crusty sourdough. I like to serve it as an appetizer at a dinner party or to my family as a more "fine dining" snack.

SERVES 10 | SERVING SIZE: ½ CUP (125 ML)

2 tbsp (30 mL) olive oil or canola oil

1 medium onion, diced

2 garlic cloves, minced

2 medium carrots, diced

2 celery stalks, diced

1 medium eggplant, cut into 1-inch (2.5 cm) pieces

1 can (14.5 oz/411 mL) no-salt-added diced tomatoes (with juice)

1 cup (250 mL) roasted red peppers, drained and chopped

⅓ cup (75 mL) pitted kalamata olives

2 tbsp (30 mL) drained capers

2 tbsp (30 mL) red wine vinegar

1 tsp (5 mL) honey

1 tsp (5 mL) dried oregano

1 tsp (5 mL) dried basil

1 tsp (5 mL) dried parsley

¼ tsp (1 mL) salt

⅛ tsp (0.5 mL) ground black pepper

1   In a large saucepan, heat the olive oil over medium heat until shimmering. Add the onion and garlic; cook, stirring occasionally, until the onion is translucent, about 3 minutes. Add the carrots and celery; cook, stirring occasionally, until softened, about 3 minutes. Add the eggplant; cook, stirring occasionally, until softened, about 10 minutes.

2   Add the diced tomatoes (with juice), roasted red peppers, olives, capers, red wine vinegar, honey, oregano, basil, parsley, salt and black pepper; stir to combine. Raise the heat to high, bring the mixture to a boil, then reduce the heat to medium. Simmer, stirring occasionally, until the flavors meld and mixture thickens, about 25 minutes. Remove from the heat and let cool slightly.

3   Spoon the caponata into a serving dish and serve immediately, or store in an airtight container in the refrigerator for up to 4 days.

Toby's Tip

To make this dish vegan, swap the honey for agave nectar.

NUTRITION INFORMATION (PER SERVING)
Calories: 70 • Total Fat: 3 g • Saturated Fat: 0 g
Protein: 1 g • Total Carbohydrates: 10 g • Fiber: 3 g
Sugars: 5 g • Sodium: 337 mg • Cholesterol: 0 mg

BAKED ZUCCHINI BITES

Looking for a warm snack you can cook up in a flash? These spiced zucchini bites take no time to prepare — though you'll probably devour them even more quickly!

SERVES 8 | SERVING SIZE: 2 TO 3 BITES

Rimmed baking sheet lined with parchment paper or a silicone mat

3 tbsp (45 mL) olive oil

1 tsp (5 mL) dried parsley

½ tsp (2 mL) paprika

½ tsp (2 mL) garlic powder

¼ tsp (1 mL) salt

2 large zucchinis (1 lb/500 g total), sliced into 1-inch (2.5 cm) rounds

2 tbsp (30 mL) grated Parmesan cheese

PREHEAT THE OVEN TO 375°F (190°C).

1 In a small bowl, whisk together the olive oil, parsley, paprika, garlic powder and salt.

2 Place the zucchini rounds on the prepared baking sheet in a single layer, spacing ½ inch (1 cm) apart. Brush the olive oil mixture over the top of each zucchini round. Sprinkle each round with an equal amount of Parmesan cheese.

3 Bake in the preheated oven until the zucchini has softened slightly and the cheese has melted, about 10 minutes. Remove from the oven and serve warm.

Toby's Tip

Swap the zucchini for summer squash.

NUTRITION INFORMATION (PER SERVING)

Calories: 69 • Total Fat: 6 g • Saturated Fat: 1 g
Protein: 3 g • Total Carbohydrates: 3 g • Fiber: 1 g
Sugars: 0 g • Sodium: 101 mg • Cholesterol: 1 mg

SOUPS

TOMATO SOUP
WITH PARMESAN CROUTONS

I like to eat this silky soup with an Avocado and White Bean Sandwich (page 99) or Veggie Chicken Salad Sandwich (page 105). If you choose to take the soup to work, add the croutons after reheating, so they stay crunchy.

SERVES 6 | SERVING SIZE: ABOUT 1¼ CUPS (310 ML)

Blender

2 tbsp (30 mL) olive oil

1 medium onion, chopped

2 garlic cloves, minced

2 cans (each 28 oz/796 mL) crushed tomatoes

2 cups (500 mL) low-sodium vegetable broth

1 tsp (5 mL) dried basil

1 tsp (5 mL) dried parsley

1 tsp (5 mL) honey or agave nectar

½ tsp (2 mL) salt

¼ tsp (1 mL) ground black pepper

1 cup (250 mL) nonfat milk

1½ cups (375 mL) Parmesan Croutons (page 186)

1 In a large saucepan, heat the oil over medium heat until shimmering. Add the onion and garlic; cook, stirring occasionally, until the onion is translucent, about 3 minutes. Add the crushed tomatoes, vegetable broth, basil, parsley, honey, salt and pepper; raise the heat to high and bring to a boil. Reduce the heat to medium-low, cover and simmer, stirring occasionally, until the flavors meld, about 30 minutes. Remove from the heat and let cool slightly.

2 Working in batches as necessary, add the cooled tomato mixture to a blender, reserving the saucepan; blend on high speed until smooth, about 1 minute.

3 In the reserved saucepan, heat the blended mixture over medium heat until simmering. Slowly stir in the milk.

4 To serve, ladle 1¼ cups (310 mL) soup into each of 6 bowls. Top each with about ¼ cup (60 mL) croutons. Serve warm.

Toby's Tip

Swap the vegetable broth for low-sodium chicken broth or water.

NUTRITION INFORMATION (PER SERVING)	Calories: 236 • Total Fat: 12 g • Saturated Fat: 2 g
	Protein: 8 g • Total Carbohydrates: 30 g • Fiber: 6 g
	Sugars: 16 g • Sodium: 868 mg • Cholesterol: 5 mg

ROASTED CARROT SOUP
WITH PESTO

This warming soup is perfect on a cold, rainy day, but it's also a gorgeous option to serve for special occasions. The swirl of green pesto pops against the bright orange of the carrot, so it's the perfect starter for when you want to impress.

SERVES 6 | SERVING SIZE: 1¼ CUPS (310 ML)

2 rimmed baking sheets lined with parchment paper or a silicone mat

Blender

2 lbs (1 kg) carrots, sliced into 1-inch (2.5 cm) rounds

3 tbsp (45 mL) olive oil, divided

½ tsp (2 mL) salt, divided

¼ tsp (1 mL) ground black pepper, divided

1 onion, chopped

2 garlic cloves, crushed

3 cups (750 mL) low-sodium vegetable broth

3 cups (750 mL) water

½ tsp (2 mL) ground coriander

¼ tsp (1 mL) ground cumin

2 tbsp (30 mL) Pesto (page 187) or store-bought

PREHEAT THE OVEN TO 400°F (200°C).

1   In a large bowl, combine the carrots, 2 tbsp (30 mL) olive oil, ¼ tsp (1 mL) salt and ⅛ tsp (0.5 mL) pepper. Spread the carrots in a single layer on the prepared baking sheets. Roast in the preheated oven, turning halfway through, until the carrots are slightly browned and fragrant, about 25 minutes. Remove from the oven and let cool for 5 minutes.

2   Meanwhile, in a large saucepan, heat the remaining 1 tbsp (15 mL) olive oil over medium heat until shimmering. Add the onion and garlic; cook, stirring occasionally, until the onion is translucent, about 3 minutes. Add the roasted carrots, vegetable broth, water, coriander, cumin and the remaining ¼ tsp (1 mL) salt and ⅛ tsp (0.5 mL) pepper; raise the heat to high and bring to a boil. Reduce the heat to medium-low, cover and simmer, stirring occasionally, until the flavors meld, about 20 minutes. Set aside to cool slightly, about 15 to 20 minutes.

3   In a blender, working in batches as necessary, blend the cooled carrot mixture on high speed until smooth, about 1 minute.

4   Ladle 1¼ cups (310 mL) soup into each of 6 bowls. Dollop 1 tsp (5 mL) pesto in each bowl and swirl it into the soup.

NUTRITION INFORMATION (PER SERVING)
Calories: 189 • Total Fat: 12 g • Saturated Fat: 2 g
Protein: 3 g • Total Carbohydrates: 20 g • Fiber: 6 g
Sugars: 9 g • Sodium: 402 mg • Cholesterol: 0 mg

TOMATO CUCUMBER GAZPACHO

Gazpacho is a summer soup meant to be served cold. I like to blend mine to make it smooth, but if you like different textures, top it with crunchy Parmesan Croutons (page 186) or crumbled Parmesan Crisps (page 186). To keep the soup vegan, sprinkle it with nutritional yeast.

SERVES 6 | SERVING SIZE: 1½ CUPS (375 ML)

Blender

2 cans (each 28 oz/796 mL) peeled whole tomatoes (with juice)

1 red bell pepper, roughly chopped

1 jalapeño pepper, seeded and roughly chopped

1 small onion, roughly chopped

1 English cucumber, peeled and chopped

2 garlic cloves, crushed

3 tbsp (45 mL) red wine vinegar

2 tbsp (30 mL) olive oil

¾ tsp (3 mL) salt

2 tbsp (30 mL) chopped fresh cilantro

1 In a blender, combine the tomatoes (with juice), bell pepper, jalapeño, onion, cucumber, garlic, red wine vinegar, olive oil and salt; blend until smooth.

2 Transfer the soup to a large bowl or container. Cover tightly and refrigerate for at least 4 hours or up to 4 days to allow the flavors to meld.

3 To serve, ladle 1½ cups (375 mL) into each of 6 soup bowls and sprinkle each with 1 tsp (5 mL) chopped cilantro.

Toby's Tip

English and hothouse cucumbers don't have seeds, so they're great for blended recipes such as soups and smoothies.

NUTRITION INFORMATION (PER SERVING)	Calories: 116 • Total Fat: 5 g • Saturated Fat: 1 g
	Protein: 3 g • Total Carbohydrates: 15 g • Fiber: 3 g
	Sugars: 9 g • Sodium: 871 mg • Cholesterol: 0 mg

CHICKEN, RICE AND ROOT VEGETABLE SOUP

This chicken soup recipe contains whole-grain brown rice and winter veggies for a fun twist. For a complete meal, serve it with crusty whole-grain bread or dinner rolls with a pat of butter.

SERVES 6 | SERVING SIZE: 1²⁄₃ CUPS (400 ML)

3 tbsp (45 mL) olive oil, divided

1 lb (500 g) boneless, skinless chicken thighs, fat trimmed, cut into 1-inch (2.5 cm) pieces

1 onion, chopped

3 garlic cloves, minced

1 celery stalk, chopped

1 carrot, peeled and chopped

2 medium turnips, peeled and chopped

3 medium parsnips, peeled and chopped

1 medium russet potato, peeled and chopped

¼ cup (60 mL) long-grain brown rice

4 cups (1 L) low-sodium chicken broth

2 cups (500 mL) water

¾ tsp (3 mL) salt

⅛ tsp (0.5 mL) ground black pepper

1 bunch fresh dill (see Toby's Tip)

1 In a large saucepan, heat 2 tbsp (30 mL) olive oil over medium heat until shimmering. Add the chicken; cook, turning once, until browned on both sides, about 6 minutes total. Using a slotted spoon, transfer the chicken to a plate, reserving the saucepan.

2 In the reserved saucepan, heat the remaining 1 tbsp (15 mL) olive oil over medium heat until shimmering. Add the onion and garlic; cook, stirring occasionally, until the onion is translucent, about 3 minutes. Add the celery, carrot, turnips, parsnips and potato; cook, stirring occasionally, until the vegetables soften, about 5 minutes. Add the cooked chicken, rice, chicken broth, water, salt, pepper and dill; raise the heat to high and bring to a boil. Reduce the heat to medium-low, cover and simmer, stirring occasionally, until the rice is tender and the flavors meld, about 35 minutes. Using tongs, carefully remove the dill and discard.

3 To serve, ladle 1²⁄₃ cups (400 mL) soup into each of 6 soup bowls. Serve warm.

Toby's Tip

To make it easier to remove the dill from the soup, use an herb bag or tie the bunch together with a silicone band.

NUTRITION INFORMATION (PER SERVING)	Calories: 363 • Total Fat: 21 g • Saturated Fat: 5 g
	Protein: 18 g • Total Carbohydrates: 27 g • Fiber: 4 g
	Sugars: 5 g • Sodium: 452 mg • Cholesterol: 74 mg

BROCCOLI CHEDDAR SOUP

This is the perfect recipe for any cheese lover. I like to use sharp (old) or extra-sharp (extra-old) Cheddar for a more prominent flavor, but any type works well here. For a complete meal, pair this soup with a salad or sandwich.

SERVES 6 | SERVING SIZE: 1⅓ CUPS (325 ML)

2 tbsp (30 mL) olive oil

1 medium onion, chopped

2 garlic cloves, minced

2 medium carrots, chopped

2 celery stalks, chopped

3 tbsp (45 mL) all-purpose flour

4 cups (1 L) low-sodium vegetable broth

1 cup (250 mL) water

4 cups (1 L) chopped broccoli

3 bay leaves

½ tsp (2 mL) smoked paprika

½ tsp (2 mL) salt

¼ tsp (1 mL) ground black pepper

⅛ tsp (0.5 mL) cayenne pepper

1 cup (250 mL) whole milk

2 cups (500 mL) shredded reduced-fat Cheddar cheese

1 In a large saucepan, heat the olive oil over medium heat until shimmering. Add the onion and garlic; cook, stirring occasionally, until the onion is translucent, about 3 minutes. Add the carrots and celery; cook, stirring occasionally, until softened, about 3 minutes.

2 Sprinkle with the flour; cook, without stirring, for 1 minute. Slowly stir in the broth and water; cook until slightly thickened, about 2 minutes. Stir in the broccoli, bay leaves, smoked paprika, salt, black pepper and cayenne pepper; raise the heat to high and bring to a boil. Reduce the heat to medium-low, cover and cook, stirring occasionally, until the broccoli has softened, about 10 minutes. Remove the bay leaves and discard.

3 Remove from the heat. Stirring constantly, slowly add the milk and then the Cheddar cheese.

4 Ladle 1⅓ cups (325 mL) soup into each of 6 bowls. Serve warm.

Toby's Tip

For a twist, substitute some of the broccoli with the same amount of chopped cauliflower.

NUTRITION INFORMATION (PER SERVING)

Calories: 230 • Total Fat: 13 g • Saturated Fat: 6 g
Protein: 15 g • Total Carbohydrates: 15 g • Fiber: 3 g
Sugars: 5 g • Sodium: 614 mg • Cholesterol: 25 mg

SPEEDY VEGETABLE SOUP

Sometimes you have very little time to whip up a meal, which is when this quick soup comes to the rescue. By using mostly canned and frozen ingredients (which are nutritious!), you can make this healthy soup in 20 minutes.

SERVES 6 | SERVING SIZE: 1½ CUPS (375 ML)

2 tbsp (30 mL) olive oil

1 medium onion, chopped

2 garlic cloves, minced

4 cups (1 L) low-sodium vegetable broth

1 can (28 oz/796 mL) crushed tomatoes

3 cups (750 mL) frozen mixed vegetables

1 can (5½ oz/156 mL) tomato paste

1 tsp (5 mL) Italian seasoning

½ tsp (2 mL) salt

⅛ tsp (0.5 mL) ground black pepper

3 cups (750 mL) lightly packed baby spinach

1 In a large saucepan, heat the olive oil over medium heat until shimmering. Add the onion and garlic; cook, stirring occasionally, until the onion is translucent, about 3 minutes. Add the vegetable broth, crushed tomatoes, mixed vegetables, tomato paste, Italian seasoning, salt and pepper; raise the heat to high and bring to a boil. Reduce the heat to medium-low, cover and simmer, stirring occasionally, for 5 minutes. Add the spinach; cook, stirring occasionally, until wilted, about 2 minutes.

2 Ladle 1½ cups (375 mL) soup into each of 6 bowls. Serve warm.

Toby's Tip

Substitute the mixed vegetables with reduced-sodium canned or frozen vegetables such as green beans, asparagus, mushrooms, peas or carrots.

NUTRITION INFORMATION (PER SERVING)	Calories: 182 • Total Fat: 5 g • Saturated Fat: 1 g Protein: 7 g • Total Carbohydrates: 31 g • Fiber: 10 g Sugars: 13 g • Sodium: 863 mg • Cholesterol: 0 mg

RATATOUILLE SOUP
WITH FARRO

Here's ratatouille in soup form, with farro for added fiber and a delicious nutty flavor.

SERVES 8 | SERVING SIZE: 1¾ CUPS (425 ML)

3 tbsp (45 mL) olive oil, divided

½ medium eggplant, cut into 1-inch (2.5 cm) pieces

½ tsp (2 mL) salt, divided

¼ tsp (1 mL) ground black pepper, divided

1 medium white onion, chopped

2 garlic cloves, minced

1 medium zucchini, cut into 1-inch (2.5 cm) pieces

1 medium yellow squash, cut into 1-inch (2.5 cm) pieces

1 red bell pepper, chopped

2 cups (500 mL) shredded green cabbage

¼ cup (60 mL) farro

4 cups (1 L) low-sodium vegetable broth

4 cups (1 L) water

1 can (14.5 oz/411 mL) no-salt-added diced tomatoes (with juice)

2 tbsp (30 mL) apple cider vinegar

½ tsp (2 mL) dried thyme

3 bay leaves

4 tsp (20 mL) capers

1   In a medium skillet, heat 1 tbsp (15 mL) olive oil over medium heat until shimmering. Add the eggplant and sprinkle with ¼ tsp (1 mL) salt and ⅛ tsp (0.5 mL) black pepper. Cook, stirring occasionally, until the eggplant is browned on all sides, about 6 minutes. Using a slotted spoon, transfer the eggplant to a bowl.

2   In a large saucepan, heat the remaining 2 tbsp (30 mL) olive oil over medium heat until shimmering. Add the onion and garlic; cook, stirring occasionally, until the onion is translucent, about 3 minutes. Add the zucchini, squash and bell pepper; cook, stirring occasionally, until softened, about 7 minutes. Add the cabbage, farro, vegetable broth, water, diced tomatoes (with juice), apple cider vinegar, thyme, bay leaves and the remaining ¼ tsp (1 mL) salt and ⅛ tsp (0.5 mL) black pepper; stir to combine. Increase the heat to high and bring the mixture to a boil. Reduce the heat to medium-low, cover and simmer, stirring occasionally, until the flavors meld, about 30 minutes. Remove the bay leaves and discard.

3   Ladle 1¾ cups (425 mL) soup into each of 8 bowls. Spoon about ½ tsp (2 mL) capers into the center of each soup. Serve warm.

NUTRITION INFORMATION (PER SERVING)
Calories: 120 • Total Fat: 6 g • Saturated Fat: 1 g
Protein: 3 g • Total Carbohydrates: 16 g • Fiber: 4 g
Sugars: 6 g • Sodium: 268 mg • Cholesterol: 0 mg

UDON NOODLE AND SHRIMP SOUP

This soup is perfect to take to work or school in an insulated container. The shrimp provide a very lean source of protein, the noodles are your carbs, and the mushrooms, carrots, green onions and cilantro have your veggies covered.

SERVES 4 | SERVING SIZE: 1⅔ CUPS (400 ML)

3 oz (90 g) dried udon noodles

1 tbsp (15 mL) olive oil

2 garlic cloves, minced

10 oz (300 g) cremini mushrooms, sliced

3 medium carrots, chopped

4 cups (1 L) low-sodium vegetable broth

2 cups (500 mL) water

½ tsp (2 mL) salt

¼ tsp (1 mL) ground ginger

¼ tsp (1 mL) ground black pepper

8 oz (250 g) raw shrimp (size 26/30), thawed if frozen, peeled and deveined

2 green onions, sliced

¼ cup (60 mL) chopped fresh cilantro

1 tbsp (15 mL) freshly squeezed lime juice

2 tsp (10 mL) reduced-sodium soy sauce

1 tsp (5 mL) sesame oil

1 Cook the noodles according to the package directions. Set aside.

2 In a large saucepan, heat the olive oil over medium heat until shimmering. Add the garlic and mushrooms; cook, stirring occasionally, until the mushrooms soften, about 5 minutes. Add the carrots; cook, stirring occasionally, until softened, about 5 minutes. Add the vegetable broth, water, salt, ginger and pepper; bring to a boil over high heat. Reduce the heat to medium-low and simmer, stirring occasionally, until the flavors combine, about 10 minutes.

3 Add the shrimp, green onions, cilantro, lime juice and soy sauce; bring to a boil over high heat. Reduce the heat to medium-low and simmer, stirring occasionally, until the shrimp are cooked through, about 2 minutes. Drizzle the sesame oil overtop.

4 To serve, ladle 1⅔ cups (400 mL) soup into each of 4 bowls. Serve immediately.

Toby's Tip

Swap all or part of the cilantro for fresh parsley or mint.

NUTRITION INFORMATION (PER SERVING)	Calories: 235 • Total Fat: 6 g • Saturated Fat: 1 g
	Protein: 18 g • Total Carbohydrates: 27 g • Fiber: 4 g
	Sugars: 5 g • Sodium: 626 mg • Cholesterol: 85 mg

SPAGHETTI AND MEATBALL SOUP

This soup is a creative spin on the popular Italian dish, but made with a warming broth. It's also a well-balanced meal, with ground meat for protein, pasta for carbs and tomato sauce as your veggie.

SERVES 6 | SERVING SIZE: 1¼ CUPS (310 ML)

MEATBALLS

12 oz (375 g) lean ground beef or pork (at least 90% lean)

⅓ cup (75 mL) panko bread crumbs

1 large egg

1 tbsp (15 mL) Worcestershire sauce

1 tsp (5 mL) Dijon mustard

1 tsp (5 mL) Italian seasoning

½ tsp (2 mL) onion powder

½ tsp (2 mL) garlic powder

¼ tsp (1 mL) salt

⅛ tsp (0.5 mL) ground black pepper

2 tbsp (30 mL) olive oil or canola oil

SOUP

1 tbsp (15 mL) olive oil or canola oil

1 medium onion, chopped

2 garlic cloves, minced

4 cups (1 L) low-sodium beef broth

1 cup (250 mL) water

1 cup (250 mL) prepared tomato sauce

2 bay leaves

¼ tsp (1 mL) salt

⅛ tsp (0.5 mL) ground black pepper

⅛ tsp (0.5 mL) hot pepper flakes

5 oz (150 g) dried spaghetti (preferably whole wheat), broken into thirds

¼ cup (60 mL) fresh basil, thinly sliced

2 tbsp (30 mL) grated Parmesan cheese

1 **MEATBALLS** In a large bowl, combine the ground beef, panko, egg, Worcestershire sauce, mustard, Italian seasoning, onion powder, garlic powder, salt and black pepper. Using clean hands, roll the mixture into balls about 1 inch (2.5 cm) in diameter and place on a plate; you should end up with about 18 meatballs. Cover and refrigerate for 15 to 30 minutes.

2 In a large saucepan, heat 2 tbsp (30 mL) olive oil over medium heat until shimmering. Working in batches as necessary, add the meatballs, cover the pan and cook, turning once, until browned on two sides, about 8 minutes total. Using a slotted spoon, remove the meatballs and transfer to a clean plate, reserving the saucepan.

3 **SOUP** In the reserved saucepan, heat 1 tbsp (15 mL) olive oil over medium heat until shimmering. Add the onion and garlic and cook, stirring occasionally, until the onion is translucent, about 3 minutes. Add the beef broth, water, tomato sauce, bay leaves, salt, black pepper, hot pepper flakes and meatballs; increase the heat to high and bring to a boil. Reduce the heat to medium-low, cover and simmer, stirring occasionally, until the flavors meld, about 20 minutes.

4 Add the spaghetti and bring to a boil over high heat. Reduce the heat to medium-low, cover partially and cook, stirring occasionally, until the spaghetti is cooked al dente, about 8 minutes. Stir in the basil and Parmesan.

5 Ladle 1¼ cups (310 mL) of the soup into each of 6 bowls. Serve warm.

NUTRITION INFORMATION (PER SERVING)	Calories: 314 • Total Fat: 14 g • Saturated Fat: 4 g
	Protein: 22 g • Total Carbohydrates: 24 g • Fiber: 2 g
	Sugars: 3 g • Sodium: 843 mg • Cholesterol: 70 mg

SPLIT PEA SOUP
WITH HAM AND BARLEY

There's a lot of nutritional goodness in this delicious pea soup. Split peas are brimming with fiber and are good sources of folate, iron and potassium. Even though split peas are a legume, they still count toward your daily recommended veggies.

SERVES 6 | SERVING SIZE: 1⅓ CUPS (325 ML)

8 cups (2 L) water

1 lb (500 g) dried split green peas

⅓ cup (75 mL) pearled barley

2 bay leaves

½ tsp (2 mL) garlic powder

½ tsp (2 mL) dried thyme

½ tsp (2 mL) dried sage

¼ tsp (1 mL) ground cumin

1 medium onion, chopped

2 medium carrots, chopped

2 celery stalks, chopped

4 oz (125 g) lean cooked ham or turkey, cut into 1-inch (2.5 cm) pieces

½ tsp (2 mL) salt

¼ tsp (1 mL) ground black pepper

1 In a large saucepan, combine the water, split peas, barley, bay leaves, garlic powder, thyme, sage and cumin; bring to a boil over high heat. Reduce the heat to medium-low, cover and simmer, stirring occasionally, about 40 minutes.

2 Add the onion, carrots and celery; increase the heat to high and bring to a boil. Reduce the heat to medium-low, cover and simmer, stirring occasionally, until the flavors combine and the peas and barley are cooked through. Add the ham, salt and pepper; bring to a boil over high heat. Reduce the heat to medium-low and stir until the ham is warmed through, about 1 minute.

3 Ladle 1⅓ cups (325 mL) soup into each of 6 bowls. Serve warm.

Toby's Tip

Look for reduced-sodium cooked ham at your deli counter.

NUTRITION INFORMATION (PER SERVING)	Calories: 353 • Total Fat: 3 g • Saturated Fat: 0 g Protein: 25 g • Total Carbohydrates: 53 g • Fiber: 10 g Sugars: 3 g • Sodium: 478 mg • Cholesterol: 13 mg

SANDWICHES

ROASTED VEGETABLE GRILLED CHEESE

Sandwiches are always a fabulous opportunity to eat your veggies, whether they are fresh or cooked. I like to use mushrooms and red pepper here, but you can add whatever leftover vegetables you have on hand. It's a delicious way to minimize food waste in the kitchen and get the most out of your money. Pair with Speedy Vegetable Soup (page 85) or Tomato Soup with Parmesan Croutons (page 76).

SERVES 4 | SERVING SIZE: 1 SANDWICH

Rimmed baking sheet lined with parchment paper or a silicone mat

Large griddle pan (optional)

1 red bell pepper, sliced into 1-inch (2.5 cm) rings

6 oz (175 g) cremini mushrooms, thinly sliced

2 tbsp (30 mL) olive oil

¼ tsp (1 mL) salt

⅛ tsp (0.5 mL) ground black pepper

8 slices crusty sourdough bread

8 tsp (40 mL) unsalted butter, softened

Nonstick cooking spray

6 oz (175 g) Havarti cheese slices, divided

PREHEAT THE OVEN TO 425°F (220°C).

1 Spread the bell pepper and mushrooms in a single layer on the prepared baking sheet. Drizzle with olive oil and sprinkle with salt and black pepper; stir to combine. Bake in the preheated oven, turning halfway through, until slightly browned, about 10 minutes.

2 Meanwhile, spread one side of each slice of bread with 1 tsp (5 mL) softened butter.

3 Coat a griddle pan or large skillet with nonstick cooking spray. Heat over medium-low heat until hot. Place 4 slices of bread, butter side down, on the pan and top each with 1 or 2 slices of cheese. Top with a layer of roasted vegetables, then an equal amount of the remaining cheese. Add a second slice of bread, butter side up. Cook until the cheese has melted and bread has browned slightly, about 5 minutes per side. Remove from the heat and slice each sandwich in half. Serve warm.

Toby's Tip

For more even cooking, press down slightly on the sandwiches with a smaller pan or the back of a spatula.

NUTRITION INFORMATION (PER SERVING)	Calories: 558 • Total Fat: 27 g • Saturated Fat: 15 g Protein: 22 g • Total Carbohydrates: 58 g • Fiber: 3 g Sugars: 4 g • Sodium: 954 mg • Cholesterol: 58 mg

AVOCADO AND WHITE BEAN SANDWICH

Avocado and white beans not only taste great together, they're super nutritious, too. Avocados provide heart-healthy monounsaturated fat, along with the carotenoids lutein and zeaxanthin, which have been shown to help keep eyes healthy as we age. Beans are filled with fiber and are a good source of iron, calcium and zinc.

SERVES 4 | SERVING SIZE: 1 SANDWICH

1¾ cups (425 mL) canned low-sodium cannellini (white kidney) or great northern beans, drained and rinsed

2 avocados, sliced

1 tbsp (15 mL) freshly squeezed lime juice

1 garlic clove, minced

2 tbsp (30 mL) chopped fresh parsley

2 tbsp (30 mL) chopped fresh cilantro

¼ tsp (1 mL) salt

⅛ tsp (0.5 mL) ground black pepper

⅛ tsp (0.5 mL) hot pepper flakes

8 slices 100% whole wheat bread, toasted

4 oz (125 g) fire-roasted red bell peppers, cut into 4 equal slices

2 mini cucumbers, thinly sliced

1   In a large bowl, mash the beans with a fork or potato masher. Add the avocado and lime juice; mash until combined. Add the garlic, parsley, cilantro, salt, black pepper and hot pepper flakes; mash until combined.

2   Place 4 slices of toasted bread on a cutting board. On each piece, lay a slice of roasted red pepper and top with ½ cup (125 mL) avocado-bean mixture. Using the back of a spoon, press down lightly. Top with cucumber slices, dividing evenly, and a second piece of toast. Slice the sandwiches in half and serve immediately.

Toby's Tip

To make this recipe gluten-free, serve the avocado-bean mixture over a salad instead of on bread.

NUTRITION INFORMATION (PER SERVING)
Calories: 412 • Total Fat: 17 g • Saturated Fat: 3 g
Protein: 17 g • Total Carbohydrates: 52 g • Fiber: 16 g
Sugars: 7 g • Sodium: 650 mg • Cholesterol: 0 mg

PITA
WITH EGGPLANT, EGG AND TAHINI

During my summers in Israel when I was young, I ate at a small hole-in-the-wall restaurant that made the most delicious sandwiches called sabich, which are made with deep-fried eggplant, hard-cooked eggs and cabbage. For a quicker, healthier version, I like to use sautéed eggplant, over-easy eggs and a refreshing chopped salad instead.

SERVES 4 | SERVING SIZE: 1 SANDWICH

EGGPLANT

2 tbsp (30 mL) olive oil

1 garlic clove, minced

½ medium eggplant, trimmed and cut into 1-inch (2.5 cm) pieces

½ tsp (2 mL) ground cumin

½ tsp (2 mL) smoked paprika

⅛ tsp (0.5 mL) salt

⅛ tsp (0.5 mL) ground black pepper

SANDWICHES

Nonstick cooking spray

4 large eggs

2 medium plum tomatoes, chopped

2 mini cucumbers, chopped

2 tbsp (30 mL) freshly squeezed lemon juice

¼ tsp (1 mL) salt

⅛ tsp (0.5 mL) ground black pepper

Four 8-inch (20 cm) whole wheat pitas, with a 1-inch (2.5 cm) strip cut off the top

½ cup (125 mL) prepared hummus

4 tsp (20 mL) tahini

1   **EGGPLANT** In a large skillet, heat the olive oil over medium heat until shimmering. Add the garlic; cook, stirring constantly, until fragrant, about 30 seconds. Add the eggplant, cumin, paprika, salt and pepper; stir, cover and cook, stirring occasionally, until softened, about 10 minutes. Transfer to a clean plate, reserving the skillet.

2   **SANDWICHES** Coat the reserved skillet with nonstick cooking spray. Heat over medium heat until hot. Add 2 eggs and cook until the edges brown, about 3 minutes. Using a spatula, carefully flip the eggs and cook until the whites are fully set, 2 to 3 minutes. Place on a clean plate. Repeat with the remaining 2 eggs.

3   In a medium bowl, combine the tomato, cucumber, lemon juice, salt and pepper.

4   To assemble the sandwiches, open a pita and place 1 cooked egg inside. Add ¼ cup (60 mL) eggplant and ½ cup (125 mL) tomato-cucumber mixture. Top with 2 tbsp (30 mL) hummus and 1 tsp (5 mL) tahini. Repeat with the remaining ingredients. Serve immediately.

**NUTRITION
INFORMATION
(PER SERVING)**

Calories: 383 • Total Fat: 19 g • Saturated Fat: 3 g
Protein: 17 g • Total Carbohydrates: 40 g • Fiber: 10 g
Sugars: 6 g • Sodium: 727 mg • Cholesterol: 186 mg

MUSHROOM CHEESESTEAK SANDWICH

This is my take on a classic cheesesteak — but vegetarian. I add tons of mushrooms, a bell pepper and onion and top it with provolone cheese. It's a warm sub that will surely become part of your regular rotation.

SERVES 4 | SERVING SIZE: 1 SANDWICH

2 tbsp (30 mL) olive oil

1 garlic clove, minced

6 oz (175 g) portobello mushrooms, cut into 1-inch (2.5 cm) slices

8 oz (250 g) cremini mushrooms, thinly sliced

1 red bell pepper, cut into 1-inch (2.5 cm) strips

½ medium onion, thinly sliced

2 tbsp (30 mL) unsalted butter

1 tsp (5 mL) dried oregano

1 tsp (5 mL) dried thyme

¼ tsp (1 mL) salt

⅛ tsp (0.5 mL) ground black pepper

¼ cup (60 mL) light mayonnaise

4 provolone cheese slices

¼ cup (60 mL) yellow mustard

Four 6-inch (15 cm) sub rolls

1 In a large skillet, heat the olive oil over medium heat until shimmering. Add the garlic and cook, stirring constantly, until fragrant, about 30 seconds. Add the portobello mushrooms, cremini mushrooms, bell pepper and onion; cook, stirring occasionally, until slightly softened, about 10 minutes. Add the butter, oregano, thyme, salt and black pepper; cook, stirring occasionally, until butter has melted. Remove from the heat.

2 On the bottom half of each roll, spread 1 tbsp (15 mL) mayonnaise. Add 1 slice of cheese, folded in half, and top with ¾ cup (175 mL) warm mushroom mixture. On the top half of each roll, spread 1 tbsp (15 mL) mustard. Press the two sides together and serve immediately.

Toby's Tip

To meal-prep this recipe, store the rolls, condiments and mushroom mixture separately. To serve, reheat the mushroom mixture and complete Step 2. You want the mushroom mixture to be warm so it will melt the cheese.

NUTRITION INFORMATION (PER SERVING)	Calories: 367 • Total Fat: 22 g • Saturated Fat: 8 g Protein: 11 g • Total Carbohydrates: 35 g • Fiber: 2 g Sugars: 8 g • Sodium: 731 mg • Cholesterol: 25 mg

ROASTED TOMATO AND TURKEY SANDWICH

Think of this recipe as a Mediterranean-inspired take on the traditional turkey sandwich. I've replaced fresh plum tomatoes with grape tomatoes roasted in seasoned olive oil.

SERVES 4 | SERVING SIZE: 1 SANDWICH

Rimmed baking sheet lined with parchment paper or a silicone mat

8 oz (250 g) grape tomatoes

2 tbsp (30 mL) olive oil

1 tsp (5 mL) Italian seasoning

¼ tsp (1 mL) salt

⅛ tsp (0.5 mL) ground black pepper

¼ cup (60 mL) light mayonnaise

1 tbsp (15 mL) Dijon mustard

8 slices 100% whole wheat bread, toasted

4 romaine lettuce leaves, halved

12 oz (375 g) lower-sodium roasted turkey breast

4 mozzarella cheese slices

PREHEAT THE OVEN TO 400°F (200°C).

1 In a medium bowl, combine the grape tomatoes, olive oil, Italian seasoning, salt and pepper; toss to coat.

2 Spoon the tomatoes onto the prepared baking sheet. Roast in the preheated oven, turning halfway through, until the tomatoes are browned, about 18 minutes. Set aside to cool slightly.

3 In a small bowl, combine the mayonnaise and mustard.

4 Place the toasted bread slices on a flat surface. Spread an equal amount of mayonnaise mixture over each slice. Top 4 bread slices with 2 lettuce halves, one-quarter of the turkey, 1 slice of cheese and about ¼ cup (60 mL) roasted tomatoes. Top with the second slice of toast. Cut each sandwich in half and serve immediately.

Toby's Tip

To reduce your sodium intake, buy low-sodium or no-salt-added turkey breast or use a smaller quantity of turkey.

NUTRITION INFORMATION (PER SERVING)	Calories: 418 • Total Fat: 19 g • Saturated Fat: 5 g
	Protein: 32 g • Total Carbohydrates: 32 g • Fiber: 6 g
	Sugars: 5 g • Sodium: 1,285 mg • Cholesterol: 71 mg

VEGGIE CHICKEN SALAD SANDWICH

I like to add additional veggies to classic salads such as chicken and tuna to help get in extra nutrients. In this chicken salad, the vegetables are finely chopped so you get delicious crunch in every bite.

SERVES 4 | SERVING SIZE: 1 SANDWICH

¼ cup (60 mL) light mayonnaise

2 tbsp (30 mL) plain nonfat Greek yogurt

1 tsp (5 mL) Dijon mustard

¼ tsp (1 mL) garlic powder

¼ tsp (1 mL) salt

⅛ tsp (0.5 mL) ground black pepper

12½ oz (390 g) canned chunk chicken breast, rinsed and drained, or diced grilled boneless, skinless breast

2 medium carrots, finely chopped

2 celery stalks, finely chopped

1 red bell pepper, finely chopped

2 tbsp (30 mL) chopped fresh parsley

4 lettuce leaves, halved

8 slices seedless rye bread

1   In a small bowl, combine the mayonnaise, Greek yogurt, mustard, garlic powder, salt and black pepper.

2   In a medium bowl, combine the chicken, carrots, celery, bell pepper and parsley. Add the mayonnaise mixture and stir to coat.

3   Place 2 lettuce leaf halves on each of 4 bread slices. Spread about ½ cup (125 mL) chicken salad onto each lettuce stack and top with a second slice of bread. Cut in half; serve.

Toby's Tip

I love my multifunctional veggie chopper, which has saved me many hours in the kitchen, not to mention that it creates evenly sized pieces. You can find many varieties online.

NUTRITION INFORMATION (PER SERVING)

Calories: 326 • Total Fat: 8 g • Saturated Fat: 1 g
Protein: 27 g • Total Carbohydrates: 37 g • Fiber: 4 g
Sugars: 5 g • Sodium: 503 mg • Cholesterol: 42 mg

BELL PEPPER SANDWICH
WITH TUNA

Swapping bread for bell pepper in a sandwich to lower carbs is also a delicious and creative way to up your veggies! For even more variety, try using Veggie Chicken Salad (page 105) instead of tuna.

SERVES 4 | SERVING SIZE: 1 WHOLE PEPPER SANDWICH

3 tbsp (45 mL) light mayonnaise

3 tbsp (45 mL) plain nonfat Greek yogurt

2 tsp (10 mL) Dijon mustard

1 tsp (5 mL) freshly squeezed lemon juice

1 tsp (5 mL) dried parsley

¼ tsp (1 mL) salt

⅛ tsp (0.5 mL) ground black pepper

1 can (10 oz/300 g) water-packed chunk light tuna, drained

½ medium red onion, chopped

1 celery stalk, chopped

4 red bell peppers, sliced in half lengthwise and cored

8 romaine lettuce leaves, halved

4 oz (125 g) Monterey Jack cheese slices, cut into 8 pieces

1   In a medium bowl, combine the mayonnaise, Greek yogurt, mustard, lemon juice, parsley, salt and black pepper. Add the tuna, onion and celery; stir to coat.

2   Lay the pepper halves on a cutting board. Place 2 lettuce halves in each and top with 2 slices of cheese. Spoon about ¼ cup (60 mL) tuna mixture on top of the cheese.

3. To serve, close 2 pepper halves together like a sandwich or eat them open-faced.

Toby's Tip

If you're trying to watch your sodium intake, choose low-sodium canned tuna or rinse the tuna before using.

NUTRITION INFORMATION (PER SERVING)
Calories: 259 • Total Fat: 13 g • Saturated Fat: 6 g
Protein: 25 g • Total Carbohydrates: 11 g • Fiber: 3 g
Sugars: 7 g • Sodium: 812 mg • Cholesterol: 59 mg

SMOKED SALMON AND VEGETABLE SLIDERS

If you're looking to up your intake of omega-3 fats without spending a lot of time in the kitchen, ready-to-eat smoked salmon is one of your best options. Omega-3 fats have been found to help decrease inflammation and the risk of heart disease. I like to serve smoked salmon on a potato roll piled high with veggies, which is a delicious way to get in several food groups.

SERVES 4 | SERVING SIZE: 1 SLIDER

½ cup (125 mL) whipped cream cheese

2 tbsp (30 mL) chopped fresh dill or ½ tsp (2 mL) dried dill

4 potato rolls, preferably whole wheat

8 oz (250 g) smoked salmon

1 medium plum tomato, thinly sliced

¼ English cucumber, thinly sliced

4 medium radishes, thinly sliced

1 In a small bowl, combine the cream cheese and dill.

2 Open up each roll and place them on a flat surface, insides facing up. Spread about 1 tbsp (15 mL) cream cheese mixture on each side of the rolls. On half of each roll, pile one-quarter of the smoked salmon and equal amounts of tomato, cucumber and radish slices. Close each sandwich and serve immediately or refrigerate for up to 2 days.

Toby's Tip

Use whatever vegetables you have on hand for this sandwich; red pepper and shredded carrot are great options. You can also pile on more tomato, cucumber and radish if you like.

NUTRITION INFORMATION (PER SERVING)

Calories: 246 • Total Fat: 11 g • Saturated Fat: 4 g

Protein: 15 g • Total Carbohydrates: 24 g • Fiber: 4 g

Sugars: 5 g • Sodium: 761 mg • Cholesterol: 33 mg

CHAPTER 7

SALADS

RED CABBAGE SLAW
WITH MANDARINS AND ALMONDS

With the hustle and bustle of everyday life, it's good to have a few go-to recipes like this one to meal prep. I love this salad because the flavors just keep getting better as it sits in the fridge during the week. Prep it on Sunday and divide it into equal portions for easy use.

SERVES 4 | SERVING SIZE: 1¼ CUPS (310 ML)

2 tbsp (30 mL) red wine vinegar

1 tsp (5 mL) agave nectar or honey

½ tsp (2 mL) garlic powder

¼ tsp (1 mL) salt

⅛ tsp (0.5 mL) ground black pepper

¼ cup (60 mL) extra-virgin olive oil

4 cups (1 L) shredded red cabbage

2 medium carrots, shredded

1 cup (250 mL) mandarin orange fruit cup or canned mandarin oranges in 100% juice or water, drained

2 green onions, sliced

¼ cup (60 mL) sliced unsalted almonds

¼ cup (60 mL) dried cranberries or dried tart cherries

1   In a small bowl, whisk together the red wine vinegar, agave nectar, garlic powder, salt and pepper. Slowly drizzle in the olive oil, whisking constantly until incorporated.

2   In a large bowl, combine the cabbage, carrots, mandarin orange pieces, green onions, almonds and dried cranberries; toss to combine.

3   Drizzle the vinegar mixture over the slaw and toss to coat. Cover and refrigerate for at least 30 minutes or up to 5 days. Serve cold.

Toby's Tip

Store extra-virgin olive oil in a cool, dark place away from any heat sources — so, not next to the stove!

NUTRITION INFORMATION (PER SERVING)	Calories: 261 • Total Fat: 17 g • Saturated Fat: 2 g Protein: 3 g • Total Carbohydrates: 26 g • Fiber: 5 g Sugars: 19 g • Sodium: 195 mg • Cholesterol: 0 mg

KALE AND CARROT SALAD

This beautifully hued salad balances the flavor of kale, a more bitter vegetable, with carrot, a sweeter one. It makes a yummy side with any sandwich or dinner dish.

SERVES 6 | SERVING SIZE: 1 CUP (250 ML)

5 cups (1.25 L) chopped Tuscan kale

1 tbsp (15 mL) freshly squeezed lemon juice

1 tsp (5 mL) olive oil

⅛ tsp (0.5 mL) salt

4 medium carrots, grated

¼ cup (60 mL) Sesame Ginger Dressing (page 198)

1   Place the kale in a large bowl. Add the lemon juice, olive oil and salt; toss to coat. Using clean hands, massage the kale with your fingers until softened, about 1 minute.

2   Add the carrots; toss to combine. Drizzle with Sesame Ginger Dressing and toss to coat. Cover and refrigerate for at least 20 minutes or up to 5 days. Serve cold.

Toby's Tip

To make this a complete meal, add 1¾ cups (425 mL) low-sodium canned chickpeas, rinsed and drained, with the carrots in Step 2.

NUTRITION INFORMATION (PER SERVING)

Calories: 132 • Total Fat: 8 g • Saturated Fat: 1 g

Protein: 3 g • Total Carbohydrates: 14 g • Fiber: 3 g

Sugars: 6 g • Sodium: 213 mg • Cholesterol: 0 mg

EASY CUCUMBER SALAD

When I was a kid, my grandmother and mother would always serve a cucumber salad for holidays. I loved it so much that I started making it for my kids, but more regularly. Now I don't have to wait to have it just twice a year!

SERVES 6 | SERVING SIZE: 1 CUP (250 ML)

Two rimmed baking sheets lined with paper towels

2 English cucumbers, sliced into ¼-inch (0.5 cm) rounds

2 tsp (10 mL) salt

¼ cup (60 mL) rice wine vinegar

2 tbsp (30 mL) chopped fresh dill

⅛ tsp (0.5 mL) ground black pepper

2 tbsp (30 mL) extra-virgin olive oil

½ medium red onion, thinly sliced

1 red bell pepper, thinly sliced

1 Spread the cucumber slices on the prepared baking sheets in a single layer. Sprinkle with salt and let stand for 1 hour.

2 Over the sink, squeeze one handful of cucumber at a time. Place the squeezed cucumber in a medium bowl.

3 In a small bowl, whisk together the rice vinegar, dill and black pepper. Slowly drizzle in the olive oil, whisking constantly until incorporated.

4 To the bowl with the cucumber, add the onion and bell pepper; toss to combine. Drizzle with the vinegar mixture and toss to coat. Cover and refrigerate for 30 minutes or up to 3 days. Serve cold.

Toby's Tip

English cucumbers, also called hothouse cucumbers, are seedless. Because they won't get soggy, they are ideal for recipes that will be refrigerated for some time. Persian, Kirby or mini cucumbers also work well in a pinch.

NUTRITION INFORMATION (PER SERVING)	Calories: 71 • Total Fat: 5 g • Saturated Fat: 1 g Protein: 2 g • Total Carbohydrates: 6 g • Fiber: 2 g Sugars: 4 g • Sodium: 198 mg • Cholesterol: 0 mg

BROCCOLI SALAD
WITH PEPITAS

Often broccoli salads are drowned in mayo, so I use a lighter combo — olive oil, light mayo, a touch of Dijon mustard and smoked paprika (for a little kick) — in this dressing. Pumpkin seeds (a.k.a. pepitas) sprinkled overtop give the salad a nice nutty, earthy flavor.

SERVES 6 | SERVING SIZE: 1 CUP (250 ML)

2 tbsp (30 mL) apple cider vinegar

2 tbsp (30 mL) light mayonnaise

2 tbsp (30 mL) extra-virgin olive oil

2 tsp (10 mL) Dijon mustard

1 tsp (5 mL) pure maple syrup

1 garlic clove, minced

¼ tsp (1 mL) smoked paprika

¼ tsp (1 mL) salt

5 cups (1.25 L) chopped trimmed broccoli (florets and stems)

½ medium red onion, chopped

¼ cup (60 mL) dried cherries or dried cranberries

2 tbsp (30 mL) toasted pumpkin seeds (pepitas)

1 In a small bowl, whisk together the apple cider vinegar, mayonnaise, olive oil, mustard, maple syrup, garlic, paprika and salt.

2 In a large bowl, combine the broccoli, onion, dried cherries and pumpkin seeds.

3 Pour the vinegar mixture over the broccoli mixture; toss to coat. Cover and refrigerate for at least 20 minutes or up to 4 days. Serve cold.

Toby's Tip

If you want your broccoli in very small pieces, use a mandoline to cut it into ⅛-inch (3 mm) slices.

NUTRITION INFORMATION (PER SERVING)

Calories: 112 • Total Fat: 6 g • Saturated Fat: 1 g

Protein: 3 g • Total Carbohydrates: 13 g • Fiber: 3 g

Sugars: 5 g • Sodium: 206 mg • Cholesterol: 1 mg

CRUNCHY FENNEL SALAD

Fennel tastes like anise, which may remind you of black licorice. It pairs beautifully with something sweet, such as mandarin oranges or apples (as in this recipe). I prefer to use sweeter apples here to balance the fennel flavor.

SERVES 6 | SERVING SIZE: 1 CUP (250 ML)

2 tbsp (30 mL) apple cider vinegar

1 tsp (5 mL) liquid honey

¼ tsp (1 mL) salt

¼ cup (60 mL) extra-virgin olive oil

1 medium bulb fennel, trimmed, quartered and thinly sliced

6 medium radishes, halved and thinly sliced

1 medium apple, such as Honeycrisp, Gala or Fuji, quartered and thinly sliced

½ cup (125 mL) roughly chopped walnuts

2 tbsp (30 mL) shredded Romano cheese

1   In a small bowl, whisk together the apple cider vinegar, honey and salt. Slowly drizzle in the olive oil, whisking constantly until incorporated.

2   In a large bowl, combine the fennel, radishes and apple. Just before serving, add the vinegar mixture and toss to coat. Top with the walnuts and Romano cheese. Serve immediately.

Toby's Tip

Swap the apple for a medium red Anjou pear.

NUTRITION INFORMATION (PER SERVING)	Calories: 134 • Total Fat: 11 g • Saturated Fat: 2 g Protein: 2 g • Total Carbohydrates: 8 g • Fiber: 2 g Sugars: 6 g • Sodium: 137 mg • Cholesterol: 2 mg

CARROT SALAD
WITH RAISINS AND APPLES

When I was growing up, my mom was the only person I knew who served sweet salads. Now that I have my own kids to feed, I try to mix it up by serving sweet salads like this one for lunch, alongside a turkey sandwich or burger.

SERVES 8 | SERVING SIZE: ½ CUP (125 ML)

¼ cup (60 mL) golden raisins

1 cup (250 mL) warm water

½ cup (125 mL) 100% apple juice

¼ cup (60 mL) freshly squeezed lemon juice

½ tsp (2 mL) vanilla extract

½ tsp (2 mL) ground cinnamon

¼ tsp (1 mL) salt

8 medium carrots, shredded

1 medium apple, such as McIntosh, Roma, Empire or Fuji, quartered and thinly sliced

1 Place the raisins in a medium bowl. Cover with the warm water and soak for 1 hour. Drain and set raisins aside.

2 In a small bowl, whisk together the apple juice, lemon juice, vanilla, cinnamon and salt.

3 In a large bowl, combine the carrots, apple and raisins. Add the apple juice mixture and toss to coat. Serve immediately.

Toby's Tip

To make an adult version of this salad, soak the raisins in the same amount of dessert wine.

NUTRITION INFORMATION (PER SERVING)

Calories: 60 • Total Fat: 0 g • Saturated Fat: 0 g
Protein: 1 g • Total Carbohydrates: 15 g • Fiber: 3 g
Sugars: 10 g • Sodium: 118 mg • Cholesterol: 0 mg

ALL GREENS SALAD
WITH LEMON VINAIGRETTE

This dynamic salad is the perfect tasty way to get in your greens! For more protein, serve it alongside a piece of cooked fish, chicken or beef, or top with sautéed diced tofu or a hard-cooked egg.

SERVES 4 | SERVING SIZE: 2¾ CUPS (675 ML)

8 oz (250 g) asparagus, trimmed and halved (see Toby's Tip)

½ cup (125 mL) frozen peas

6 cups (1.5 L) chopped romaine lettuce

2 tbsp (30 mL) chopped fresh dill

½ English cucumber, cut lengthwise and sliced into ½-inch (1 cm) half-moons

1 green bell pepper, cut into 1-inch (2.5 cm) strips

1 avocado, thinly sliced

½ cup (125 mL) Lemon Vinaigrette (page 195)

1 Add 1 inch (2.5 cm) water to a medium saucepan fitted with a steamer basket. Place the asparagus in the basket and bring the water to a boil over high heat. Reduce the heat to low, cover and steam until the asparagus is just tender, about 8 minutes. Using tongs, remove the asparagus from the steamer basket and transfer to a medium bowl.

2 Remove the steamer basket from the saucepan. Add water as necessary to maintain 1 inch (2.5 cm) in the pan; bring to a boil over high heat. Add the peas and cook until tender, about 5 minutes. Drain and add to the bowl with the asparagus.

3 In a large serving bowl, combine the lettuce and dill. Add the cucumber, bell pepper, cooked asparagus and peas. Just before serving, top with the avocado and add the Lemon Vinaigrette; toss to coat.

Toby's Tip

If your asparagus spears are quite thin, the cooking time may be shortened by a few minutes.

NUTRITION INFORMATION (PER SERVING)
Calories: 292 • Total Fat: 26 g • Saturated Fat: 4 g
Protein: 5 g • Total Carbohydrates: 15 g • Fiber: 8 g
Sugars: 4 g • Sodium: 170 mg • Cholesterol: 0 mg

CHICKPEA SALAD
WITH COUSCOUS

This salad includes chickpeas — also called garbanzo beans — which count toward your daily recommended vegetable intake. In this recipe I combine them with couscous to make it heartier, and a few other veggies for crunch and flavor. I use Tahini Dressing here, but you can try the Red Wine Vinaigrette (page 194) or Lemon Vinaigrette (page 195) instead.

SERVES 6 | SERVING SIZE: ABOUT 1 CUP (250 ML)

1½ cups (375 mL) water

1 cup (250 mL) pearl couscous

Four 2-inch (5 cm) strips lemon rind

1¾ cups (425 mL) low-sodium canned chickpeas, drained and rinsed

½ English cucumber, chopped

1 cup (250 mL) cherry tomatoes, halved

2 tbsp (30 mL) chopped fresh parsley

½ cup (125 mL) Tahini Dressing (page 198)

¼ cup (60 mL) crumbled goat cheese

1 In a medium saucepan, bring the water, couscous and lemon rind to a boil over high heat. Reduce the heat to low and simmer until the couscous is tender, about 15 minutes. Drain, stir and set aside to cool for 10 minutes. Discard the lemon rind.

2 In a large bowl, combine the cooled couscous, chickpeas, cucumber, tomatoes and parsley. Add the Tahini Dressing; toss to coat. Sprinkle with the goat cheese. Serve immediately.

Toby's Tip

Swap the chickpeas for the same amount of great northern beans or cannellini (white kidney) beans.

NUTRITION INFORMATION (PER SERVING) Calories: 270 • Total Fat: 10 g • Saturated Fat: 2 g
Protein: 9 g • Total Carbohydrates: 38 g • Fiber: 5 g
Sugars: 5 g • Sodium: 297 mg • Cholesterol: 3 mg

GREEK SALAD
WITH EDAMAME

Traditional Greek salad may be famous, but it doesn't have enough protein to keep you satisfied. In come edamame, also known as baby soybeans! This plant-based protein powerhouse is easy to use if you cook them from frozen (it takes only 5 minutes!), so I always keep a bag in the freezer.

SERVES 4 | SERVING SIZE: 1¾ CUPS (425 ML)

---

1 cup (250 mL) frozen shelled edamame

5 cups (1.25 L) lightly packed Bibb or butter lettuce, cut into bite-size pieces

1 medium plum tomato, cut lengthwise and sliced into half-moons

½ English cucumber, cut lengthwise and sliced into half-moons

6 medium radishes, quartered

¼ cup (60 mL) kalamata olives, pitted and halved

¼ cup (60 mL) Balsamic Vinaigrette (page 194) or store-bought

¼ cup (60 mL) crumbled feta cheese

1 Fill a small saucepan three-quarters full with water; bring to a boil over high heat. Add the edamame, reduce the heat to medium-low and simmer until tender, about 5 minutes. Drain and let cool for 10 minutes.

2 Meanwhile, in a large bowl, combine the lettuce, tomato, cucumber, radishes and olives. Add the Balsamic Vinaigrette and toss to coat. Sprinkle with feta cheese. Serve immediately.

Toby's Tip

Swap the edamame for 12 oz (375 g) chopped grilled chicken or shrimp.

NUTRITION INFORMATION (PER SERVING)	Calories: 175 • Total Fat: 14 g • Saturated Fat: 2 g Protein: 6 g • Total Carbohydrates: 9 g • Fiber: 3 g Sugars: 5 g • Sodium: 467 mg • Cholesterol: 8 mg

LENTIL SALAD
WITH CHOPPED VEGETABLES

Lentils are an easy plant-based protein to add to salads. You can take this salad to work and enjoy it as a main dish with a whole wheat roll or a crusty piece of bread.

SERVES 4 | SERVING SIZE: 2 CUPS (500 ML)

4 cups (1 L) fresh arugula

1 cup (250 mL) canned brown lentils, drained and rinsed

1 English cucumber, chopped

1 cup (250 mL) cherry tomatoes, halved

¼ medium red onion, chopped

¼ cup (60 mL) Red Wine Vinaigrette (page 194) or store-bought

¼ cup (60 mL) crumbled feta cheese

2 tbsp (30 mL) sliced almonds

1 In a large bowl, combine the arugula, lentils, cucumber, tomatoes and onion. Drizzle the Red Wine Vinaigrette over the salad; toss to coat. Sprinkle with feta cheese and almonds. Serve immediately.

Toby's Tip

Swap the lentils for black beans or pinto beans.

NUTRITION INFORMATION (PER SERVING)	Calories: 209 • Total Fat: 13 g • Saturated Fat: 3 g
	Protein: 9 g • Total Carbohydrates: 17 g • Fiber: 6 g
	Sugars: 5 g • Sodium: 174 mg • Cholesterol: 8 mg

SOBA NOODLE SALAD
WITH VEGETABLES AND GRILLED TOFU

Soba noodles are thin Japanese noodles made from buckwheat. They have a nutty flavor and a dense texture and can be enjoyed hot or cold. I love them in this dish with the filling tofu and a variety of veggies.

SERVES 4 | SERVING SIZE: 2 CUPS (500 ML)

8 oz (250 g) dried soba noodles

¼ cup (60 mL) olive oil, divided

3 tbsp (45 mL) freshly squeezed lime juice

½ tsp (2 mL) chili powder

½ tsp (2 mL) dried cilantro

½ tsp (2 mL) garlic powder

½ tsp (2 mL) salt, divided

8 oz (250 g) extra-firm tofu, cut into 1-inch (2.5 cm) cubes

Nonstick cooking spray

4 cups (1 L) lightly packed baby spinach

½ English cucumber, chopped

2 medium carrots, grated

1 Fill a large pot three-quarters full with water and bring to a boil over high heat. Add the soba noodles, reduce the heat to medium and cook until tender, about 8 minutes. Drain and run under cold water. Place in a large bowl and set aside to cool slightly.

2 Meanwhile, in a small bowl, whisk together 3 tbsp (45 mL) olive oil, lime juice, chili powder, cilantro, garlic powder and ¼ tsp (1 mL) salt. Set aside.

3 Place the tofu in a medium bowl. Add 2 tbsp (30 mL) of the lime juice mixture; toss to coat. Cover the bowl and place in the refrigerator for 30 minutes or up to 24 hours.

4 Coat a large skillet with nonstick cooking spray. Heat over medium heat until hot. Add the tofu, discarding the marinade, and cook, turning once, until golden brown, about 5 minutes total. Transfer to a clean plate, reserving the skillet.

5 In the reserved skillet, heat the remaining 1 tbsp (15 mL) olive oil over medium heat until shimmering. Add the spinach and remaining ¼ tsp (1 mL) salt; cook, stirring occasionally, until wilted, about 3 minutes.

6 In the large bowl, combine the soba noodles, tofu, cooked spinach, cucumber and carrots. Add the remaining lime juice mixture and toss to coat. Serve immediately.

Toby's Tip

Add more veggies to this salad, especially if you have some you need to use up. Radishes, additional cucumber, green onions and cooked mushrooms all work well.

NUTRITION INFORMATION (PER SERVING)	Calories: 405 • Total Fat: 17 g • Saturated Fat: 2 g
	Protein: 13 g • Total Carbohydrates: 52 g • Fiber: 6 g
	Sugars: 5 g • Sodium: 382 mg • Cholesterol: 0 mg

LEMON ORZO SALAD
WITH PEAS AND SALMON

This meal-in-a-bowl combines salmon, orzo and lots of veggies to make a refreshingly light lunch. Round it out with some fresh fruit, such as clementines, pears or grapes.

SERVES 4 | SERVING SIZE: 1¼ CUPS (310 ML)

Rimmed baking sheet, lined with parchment paper or a silicone mat

1 salmon fillet (1 lb/500 g)	1 tbsp (15 mL) olive oil
¼ tsp (1 mL) salt	4 cups (1 L) lightly packed baby spinach
⅛ tsp (0.5 mL) ground black pepper	1 cup (250 mL) cherry tomatoes, halved
4 oz (125 g) orzo pasta, preferably whole wheat	¼ cup (60 mL) Lemon Vinaigrette (page 195) or store-bought
1 cup (250 mL) frozen peas	2 tbsp (30 mL) grated Parmesan cheese

PREHEAT THE OVEN TO 425°F (220°C).

1 Sprinkle the flesh side of the salmon with the salt and pepper. Place on the prepared baking sheet and roast in the preheated oven until the internal temperature of the fish reaches 145°F (63°C), about 12 to 15 minutes. Transfer the cooked salmon to a cutting board and let cool for 10 minutes.

2 Using a fork, break off bite-size pieces of salmon, discarding the skin, and place in a large bowl.

3 Meanwhile, fill a medium saucepan three-quarters full with water; bring to a boil over high heat. Add the orzo; cook for 2 minutes. Add the peas and cook for 5 to 6 minutes more, until the orzo is al dente. Drain and let cool for 10 minutes.

4 Meanwhile, in a large skillet, heat the olive oil over medium heat until shimmering. Add the spinach; cook, stirring occasionally, until wilted, about 3 minutes. Set aside to cool slightly.

5 To the salmon in the large bowl, add the cooled orzo, peas, spinach and tomatoes; toss to combine. Add the Lemon Vinaigrette and toss to coat. Sprinkle with Parmesan cheese. Serve immediately.

Toby's Tip

If you want to add crunch to your salad, add 2 tbsp (30 mL) pine nuts in Step 5.

NUTRITION INFORMATION (PER SERVING)	Calories: 488 • Total Fat: 27 g • Saturated Fat: 6 g Protein: 31 g • Total Carbohydrates: 29 g • Fiber: 8 g Sugars: 3 g • Sodium: 416 mg • Cholesterol: 65 mg

ROASTED TOMATO AND SHRIMP SALAD

This protein-filled salad is made with very lean shrimp roasted with tomatoes in a light olive oil–based seasoning and tossed over lots of veggies. It's a healthy meal for lunch or to enjoy for dinner on a busy work night.

SERVES 4 | SERVING SIZE: 2¼ CUPS (560 ML) SALAD
+ 1 CUP (250 ML) SHRIMP MIXTURE

Rimmed baking sheet lined with parchment paper or a silicone mat

12 oz (375 g) raw shrimp (size 31/40), thawed if frozen, peeled and deveined

10 oz (300 g) grape tomatoes, halved

2 tbsp (30 mL) olive oil

1 tsp (5 mL) Italian seasoning

¼ tsp (1 mL) garlic powder

¼ tsp (1 mL) salt

⅛ tsp (0.5 mL) ground black pepper

6 cups (1.5 L) chopped romaine lettuce

½ English cucumber, cut lengthwise and sliced into 1-inch (2.5 cm) half-moons

1 yellow bell pepper, sliced into 1-inch (2.5 cm) strips

4 oz (125 g) low-moisture mozzarella cheese, cut into 1-inch (2.5 cm) cubes

½ cup (125 mL) Lemon Vinaigrette (page 195)

PREHEAT THE OVEN TO 350°F (180°C).

1   In a large bowl, combine the shrimp and tomatoes. Add the olive oil, Italian seasoning, garlic powder, salt and black pepper; toss to coat. Gently spread the mixture on the prepared baking sheet in a single layer. Place in the preheated oven and roast until the shrimp are opaque, 10 to 12 minutes.

2   In a separate large bowl, combine the lettuce, cucumber, bell pepper and mozzarella cheese; top with the roasted shrimp-tomato mixture. Just before serving, add the Lemon Vinaigrette and toss to coat. Serve immediately.

Toby's Tip

Swap the Lemon Vinaigrette for Balsamic Vinaigrette (page 194) or a store-bought balsamic vinaigrette.

NUTRITION INFORMATION (PER SERVING)	Calories: 429 • Total Fat: 33 g • Saturated Fat: 8 g
	Protein: 26 g • Total Carbohydrates: 11 g • Fiber: 3 g
	Sugars: 4 g • Sodium: 600 mg • Cholesterol: 162 mg

CAESAR SALAD
WITH GRILLED COD

Most restaurants will offer a Caesar salad served with grilled chicken or shrimp. But what about cod? It's a flaky, mild-flavored white fish that is easy to find and to cook. The cod adds a healthy amount of lean protein to your salad, while the dressing adds a delicious creamy note.

SERVES 4 | SERVING SIZE: ABOUT 2 CUPS (500 ML)

8 cups (2 L) romaine lettuce, roughly chopped

¼ cup (60 mL) grated Parmesan cheese

1 cup (250 mL) Parmesan Croutons (page 186) or store-bought

1 lb (500 g) cod, cut into 4 fillets

¼ tsp (1 mL) salt

⅛ tsp (0.5 mL) ground black pepper

Nonstick cooking spray

½ cup (125 mL) Caesar Dressing (page 199) or store-bought

1 In a large bowl, combine the lettuce, Parmesan cheese and croutons. Set aside.

2 Sprinkle both sides of the cod with the salt and pepper.

3 Coat a large grill pan or skillet with nonstick cooking spray. Heat over medium heat until hot. Add the cod, cover and cook, turning once, until its internal temperature reaches 145°F (63°C), about 6 to 8 minutes.

4 Spoon about 2 cups (500 mL) salad into each of 4 bowls. Drizzle about 2 tbsp (30 mL) Caesar Dressing over each and top with one cooked cod fillet. Serve immediately.

Toby's Tip

You can also cook the cod on an outdoor grill. Preheat the grill and brush the grates with olive oil. Cook the cod for 6 to 8 minutes, turning once, until its internal temperature reaches 145°F (63°C).

NUTRITION INFORMATION (PER SERVING)	Calories: 283 • Total Fat: 14 g • Saturated Fat: 4 g
	Protein: 29 g • Total Carbohydrates: 10 g • Fiber: 3 g
	Sugars: 3 g • Sodium: 593 mg • Cholesterol: 61 mg

BLT SALAD
WITH CHICKEN

This recipe turns the popular BLT sandwich into a salad but includes even more protein — chicken breast! You can serve crusty bread alongside for some extra carbs if you like, or leave it out; the choice is yours.

SERVES 6 | SERVING SIZE: 1²/₃ CUPS (400 ML)

1 lb (500 g) boneless, skinless chicken breast cutlets

¼ tsp (1 mL) salt

⅛ tsp (0.5 mL) ground black pepper

2 tbsp (30 mL) olive oil

4 slices bacon or turkey bacon

4 cups (1 L) shredded romaine lettuce

1 cup (250 mL) cherry tomatoes, halved

1 cup (250 mL) Parmesan Croutons (page 186) or store-bought

¼ medium red onion, thinly sliced

½ cup (125 mL) Lighter Buttermilk Dressing (page 195) or store-bought

1 Sprinkle both sides of each chicken cutlet with the salt and pepper.

2 In a large skillet, heat the olive oil over medium heat until shimmering. Working in batches as necessary, add the cutlets and cook until their internal temperature reaches 165°F (74°C), about 5 minutes on each side. Place on a cutting board to cool slightly, reserving the skillet, then cut into 1-inch (2.5 cm) pieces.

3 Heat the reserved skillet over medium heat until hot. Add the bacon and cook, turning frequently, until crispy, about 10 to 12 minutes. Transfer to a plate lined with paper towels. Set aside to cool for 10 minutes, then chop.

4 In a large bowl, combine the lettuce, cooked chicken, tomatoes, Parmesan Croutons, onion and cooked bacon. Just before serving, add the Lighter Buttermilk Dressing and toss to coat.

Toby's Tip

Swap the bacon for avocado.

NUTRITION INFORMATION (PER SERVING)	Calories: 290 • Total Fat: 19 g • Saturated Fat: 4 g
	Protein: 22 g • Total Carbohydrates: 7 g • Fiber: 2 g
	Sugars: 3 g • Sodium: 514 mg • Cholesterol: 69 mg

Toby's Tip

Swap the grouper for mahi-mahi, cod or flounder. Just watch your cooking time: thinner fish take less time to cook, while thicker fish take a few minutes longer.

PANZANELLA SALAD
WITH MOZZARELLA AND GROUPER

Up your salad game with this mouthwatering salad that's filled with tons of veggies, mozzarella cheese and crunchy croutons — all topped with lemony-flavored grouper. It's also an easy dinner to prepare in about 45 minutes.

SERVES 6 | SERVING SIZE: 1 BOWL

Rimmed baking sheet lined with parchment paper or a silicone mat

3 tbsp (45 mL) olive oil

2 lemons, divided

1 tsp (5 mL) Italian seasoning

1/2 tsp (2 mL) onion powder

1/2 tsp (2 mL) garlic powder

1/4 tsp (1 mL) salt

1/8 tsp (0.5 mL) ground black pepper

2 lbs (1 kg) grouper, cut into 6 fillets

4 cups (1 L) shredded romaine lettuce

1 cup (250 mL) cherry tomatoes, halved

1 yellow bell pepper, cut into 1-inch (2.5 cm) strips

1/2 English cucumber, cut lengthwise and sliced into 1/2-inch (1 cm) half-moons

1/4 small red onion, thinly sliced

1/4 cup (60 mL) fresh basil leaves, sliced into 1/4-inch (0.5 cm) ribbons

4 oz (125 g) fresh mozzarella cheese, cut into 1-inch (2.5 cm) cubes

1 cup (250 mL) Parmesan Croutons (page 186) or store-bought

3/4 cup (175 mL) Balsamic Vinaigrette (page 194) or store-bought

1 In a medium bowl, whisk together the olive oil, zest and juice of 1 lemon, Italian seasoning, onion powder, garlic powder, salt and black pepper. Add the grouper fillets and turn to coat. Cover and refrigerate for at least 30 minutes or up to 2 hours.

2 Preheat the oven to 400°F (200°C).

3 Remove the fish from the marinade and place on the prepared baking sheet. Thinly slice the remaining lemon. Arrange the lemon slices on top of the fillets. Bake until the fish is flaky and its internal temperature reaches 145°F (63°C), about 15 to 17 minutes.

4 In a large bowl, combine the lettuce, tomatoes, bell pepper, cucumber, onion, basil, mozzarella cheese and Parmesan Croutons.

5 Spoon 1 1/2 cups (375 mL) salad into each of 6 bowls. Drizzle about 2 tbsp (30 mL) Balsamic Vinaigrette over each and top with one cooked grouper fillet. Serve immediately.

NUTRITION INFORMATION (PER SERVING)	Calories: 455 • Total Fat: 29 g • Saturated Fat: 6 g
	Protein: 37 g • Total Carbohydrates: 13 g • Fiber: 3 g
	Sugars: 6 g • Sodium: 536 mg • Cholesterol: 72 mg

KALE AND SWEET POTATO SALAD
WITH SHREDDED CHICKEN

Kale is part of the cabbage family and has a slightly peppery taste that complements the sweet flavor of the potatoes. Add chicken for protein and pecans for healthy fat and crunch, and you've got a delicious all-in-one meal.

SERVES 4 | SERVING SIZE: 2 CUPS (500 ML)

Rimmed baking sheet lined with parchment paper or a silicone mat

2 tbsp (30 mL) + 1 tsp (5 mL) olive oil, divided

2 tsp (10 mL) balsamic vinegar

¼ tsp (1 mL) garlic powder

¼ tsp (1 mL) + ⅛ tsp (0.5 mL) salt, divided

⅛ tsp (0.5 mL) ground black pepper

1 medium sweet potato, peeled and cut into 1-inch (2.5 cm) pieces

½ sweet onion, thinly sliced

¼ cup (60 mL) raw pecans, chopped

4 cups (1 L) lightly packed chopped Tuscan kale

1 tbsp (15 mL) freshly squeezed lemon juice

2 cups (500 mL) shredded rotisserie chicken or chopped grilled chicken

½ cup (125 mL) Balsamic Vinaigrette (page 194) or store-bought

PREHEAT THE OVEN TO 425°F (220°C).

1   In a medium bowl, whisk together 2 tbsp (30 mL) olive oil, balsamic vinegar, garlic powder, ¼ tsp (1 mL) salt and pepper. Add the sweet potato and onion; toss to coat. Transfer the mixture to the prepared baking sheet and spread it out in a single layer. Roast in the preheated oven, turning halfway through, until golden brown, about 18 minutes.

2   Meanwhile, heat a small skillet over medium-low heat. Once the skillet is hot, add the pecans and toast, tossing regularly, until golden brown, about 5 minutes. Remove from the heat and let cool for 10 minutes.

3   In a large bowl, combine the kale, lemon juice, remaining 1 tsp (5 mL) olive oil and remaining ⅛ tsp (0.5 mL) salt. Using clean hands, massage the kale until softened, about 1 minute. Add the cooked vegetables and the chicken. Just before serving, drizzle with Balsamic Vinaigrette; toss to coat. Sprinkle with the toasted pecans. Serve immediately.

NUTRITION INFORMATION (PER SERVING)	Calories: 478 • Total Fat: 29 g • Saturated Fat: 4 g Protein: 26 g • Total Carbohydrates: 32 g • Fiber: 6 g Sugars: 11 g • Sodium: 713 mg • Cholesterol: 62 mg

Toby's Tip

If you like cheese in your salad, add ¼ cup (60 mL) crumbled goat cheese or blue cheese.

Toby's Tip

Swap the chicken for tofu cut into 1-inch (2.5 cm) pieces. Bake, turning halfway and brushing with the reserved marinade, until crispy, about 10 minutes.

BARBECUE-STYLE CHICKEN SALAD

In this recipe you get all the flavors of a cookout barbecue in one delicious salad.

SERVES 6 | SERVING SIZE: 1²⁄₃ CUPS (400 ML)

Rimmed baking sheet lined with parchment paper or a silicone mat

BARBECUE-STYLE CHICKEN

¾ cup (175 mL) ketchup

4 tsp (20 mL) apple cider vinegar

2 tbsp (30 mL) brown sugar

1 tbsp (15 mL) Worcestershire sauce

1 garlic clove, minced

2 tsp (10 mL) smoked paprika

⅛ tsp (0.5 mL) salt

1 lb (500 g) boneless, skinless chicken breasts

SALAD

4 cups (1 L) shredded romaine lettuce

2 medium plum tomatoes, chopped

1 cup (250 mL) low-sodium canned black beans, drained and rinsed

1 cup (250 mL) canned corn, drained and rinsed

1 avocado, thinly sliced

⅓ cup (75 mL) shredded reduced-fat Cheddar cheese

½ cup (125 mL) Cilantro-Lime Dressing (page 196) or store-bought

1 **BARBECUE-STYLE CHICKEN** In a medium bowl, whisk together the ketchup, apple cider vinegar, brown sugar, Worcestershire sauce, garlic, paprika and salt. Transfer ¼ cup (60 mL) of the marinade to a small bowl and reserve.

2 Place the chicken breasts in the medium bowl; turn to coat with marinade. Cover and refrigerate for at least 30 minutes or up to 24 hours.

3 Preheat the oven to 425°F (220°C).

4 Remove the chicken from the marinade, shake off excess and place on the prepared baking sheet. Discard the chicken marinade. Bake in the preheated oven for 15 minutes.

5 Remove the chicken from the oven and brush with the reserved ¼ cup (60 mL) marinade. Return to the oven and cook until its internal temperature reaches 165°F (74°C), about 15 minutes more. Remove from the oven and let cool slightly for 10 minutes, then cut into 1-inch (2.5 cm) slices.

6 **SALAD** In a large bowl, combine the lettuce, tomatoes, black beans, corn and chicken. Top with avocado and Cheddar cheese. Just before serving, add the Cilantro-Lime Dressing and toss to coat. Serve immediately.

NUTRITION INFORMATION (PER SERVING)	Calories: 458 • Total Fat: 30 g • Saturated Fat: 5 g
	Protein: 24 g • Total Carbohydrates: 27 g • Fiber: 7 g
	Sugars: 11 g • Sodium: 611 mg • Cholesterol: 59 mg

EASY ROTISSERIE CHICKEN SALAD

Rotisserie chicken can come to the rescue on a busy weeknight. In this recipe I combine it with veggies (spinach, cucumber and tomatoes) and proteins in the form of feta cheese and pistachios. It's a salad that can be whipped up in a flash.

SERVES 6 | SERVING SIZE: 1½ CUPS (375 ML)

4 cups (1 L) baby spinach

2 cups (500 mL) shredded rotisserie chicken or diced leftover chicken

1 cup (250 mL) cherry tomatoes, halved

½ English cucumber, cut lengthwise and sliced into ½-inch (1 cm) half-moons

¼ cup (60 mL) jarred sliced pickled pepperoncini

¼ small red onion, thinly sliced

½ cup (125 mL) crumbled feta cheese

¼ cup (60 mL) pistachios, chopped

¾ cup (175 mL) Lemon Vinaigrette (page 195) or store-bought

1 In a large bowl, combine the spinach, chicken, tomatoes, cucumber, pepperoncini and red onion. Sprinkle with the feta cheese and pistachios. Just before serving, add the Lemon Vinaigrette and toss to coat.

Toby's Tip

Swap the chicken for 8 oz (250 g) cooked shrimp or sliced salmon.

NUTRITION INFORMATION (PER SERVING)

Calories: 314 • Total Fat: 25 g • Saturated Fat: 5 g

Protein: 18 g • Total Carbohydrates: 7 g • Fiber: 2 g

Sugars: 2 g • Sodium: 490 mg • Cholesterol: 53 mg

CHEESEBURGER SALAD

This bun-less cheeseburger-in-a-bowl was inspired by the Big Mac, and it will be a hit in your home just as it is in mine. It's basically all the deliciousness of the famous burger — ground beef, cheese, pickles, tomatoes, lettuce, dressing — but in a salad!

SERVES 6 | SERVING SIZE: 1²⁄₃ CUPS (400 ML)

1 lb (500 g) ground beef, at least 90% lean

1 large egg, beaten

½ cup (125 mL) panko bread crumbs

2 tbsp (30 mL) low-fat milk

1 tbsp (15 mL) Worcestershire sauce

1 tsp (5 mL) Italian seasoning

½ tsp (2 mL) garlic powder

½ tsp (2 mL) onion powder

¼ tsp (1 mL) salt

⅛ tsp (0.5 mL) ground black pepper

2 tbsp (30 mL) olive oil

4 cups (1 L) shredded romaine lettuce

2 medium plum tomatoes, thinly sliced

¼ medium red onion, thinly sliced

3 dill pickles, thinly sliced

½ cup (125 mL) shredded reduced-fat Cheddar cheese

¾ cup (175 mL) Lighter Thousand Island Dressing (page 199) or store-bought

1. In a large bowl, combine the ground beef, egg, panko, milk, Worcestershire sauce, Italian seasoning, garlic powder, onion powder, salt and pepper. Using clean hands, mix until just combined. Divide the mixture into 4 equal amounts, roll into balls and shape into hamburger patties. Place on a clean plate, cover and refrigerate for 20 to 30 minutes.

2. In a large skillet, heat the olive oil over medium heat until shimmering. Add the patties, cover and cook until their internal temperature reaches 155°F (68°C), about 4 minutes on each side. Transfer to a cutting board and let cool for 10 minutes. Cut each patty into 6 pieces.

3. Meanwhile, in a separate large bowl, combine the lettuce, hamburger pieces, tomatoes, onion and pickles. Sprinkle with the Cheddar cheese. Just before serving, add the Lighter Thousand Island Dressing and toss to coat.

NUTRITION INFORMATION (PER SERVING)

Calories: 294 • Total Fat: 17 g • Saturated Fat: 6 g
Protein: 22 g • Total Carbohydrates: 12 g • Fiber: 2 g
Sugars: 5 g • Sodium: 781 mg • Cholesterol: 89 mg

TACO SALAD

One of my kids' favorite dinners is taco night, but if you want to mix it up, why not try a taco salad, sans the tortilla? The ground beef is cooked in a delicious homemade taco seasoning and then tossed in a salad packed with veggies and protein. You can even add 1 ounce (30 g) of crushed tortilla chips for some more crunch!

SERVES 6 | SERVING SIZE: 1²⁄₃ CUPS (400 ML)

¼ tsp (1 mL) salt

¼ tsp (1 mL) chili powder

¼ tsp (1 mL) smoked paprika

¼ tsp (1 mL) ground cumin

¼ tsp (1 mL) onion powder

¼ tsp (1 mL) garlic powder

¼ tsp (1 mL) dried oregano

2 tbsp (30 mL) olive oil

12 oz (375 g) ground beef, at least 90% lean

4 cups (1 L) shredded romaine lettuce

1 cup (250 mL) cherry tomatoes, halved

1 cup (250 mL) low-sodium canned black beans, drained and rinsed

2 medium green onions, chopped

½ cup (125 mL) shredded reduced-fat Cheddar cheese

1 avocado, thinly sliced

¾ cup (175 mL) Cilantro-Lime Dressing (page 196) or store-bought

1 In a small bowl, combine the salt, chili powder, paprika, cumin, onion powder, garlic powder and oregano.

2 In a medium skillet, heat the olive oil over medium heat until shimmering. Add the ground beef and sprinkle with the spice mixture. Cook, breaking up the meat with a wooden spoon, until it's cooked through, about 8 minutes. Set aside to cool slightly.

3 In a large bowl, combine the lettuce, cooked ground beef, tomatoes, black beans and green onions. Sprinkle with the Cheddar cheese and top with avocado slices. Just before serving, add the Cilantro-Lime Dressing and toss to coat.

Toby's Tip

Swap the ground beef for the seitan version, which is plant-based.

NUTRITION INFORMATION (PER SERVING)
Calories: 442 • Total Fat: 38 g • Saturated Fat: 8 g
Protein: 17 g • Total Carbohydrates: 13 g • Fiber: 6 g
Sugars: 2 g • Sodium: 441 mg • Cholesterol: 42 mg

BALSAMIC PORK TENDERLOIN SALAD
WITH STRAWBERRIES

When you opt to eat meat, try to choose leaner cuts such as pork tenderloin. It's the leanest cut of pork around, as lean as boneless, skinless chicken breast! This combination of pork, spring greens, sweet strawberries and black olives makes an incredibly delicious and satisfying meal.

SERVES 6 | SERVING SIZE: 1²/₃ CUPS (400 ML)

Rimmed baking sheet lined with a silicone mat

1 lb (500 g) pork tenderloin

½ cup (125 mL) Balsamic Vinaigrette (page 194) or store-bought, divided

4 cups (1 L) mixed spring greens

2 cups (500 mL) strawberries, sliced

1 cup (250 mL) pitted black olives, halved

⅓ cup (75 mL) crumbled goat cheese

1 In a large bowl, combine the pork tenderloin and about ¼ cup (60 mL) Balsamic Vinaigrette; turn to coat. Cover and refrigerate for at least 1 hour or up to 24 hours.

2 Preheat the oven to 400°F (200°C).

3 Transfer the pork to the prepared baking sheet, discarding the marinade. Cook in the preheated oven until a thermometer inserted into the thickest part of the meat reads 145°F (63°C), about 40 minutes. Transfer the pork to a cutting board and let stand for 10 minutes. Cut into 1-inch (2.5 cm) slices.

4 Place the spring greens in a large bowl. Place the pork slices, strawberries and olives on top. Sprinkle with goat cheese. Just before serving, add the remaining ¼ cup (60 mL) Balsamic Vinaigrette and toss to coat.

Toby's Tip

Swap the pork for boneless, skinless chicken breasts. In Step 3, cook the chicken for about 20 to 25 minutes, until its internal temperature reaches 165°F (74°C).

NUTRITION INFORMATION (PER SERVING)	Calories: 239 • Total Fat: 15 g • Saturated Fat: 4 g
	Protein: 18 g • Total Carbohydrates: 9 g • Fiber: 2 g
	Sugars: 5 g • Sodium: 494 mg • Cholesterol: 41 mg

TUNA NIÇOISE SALAD

This salad is a heartier version of a classic niçoise.

SERVES 4 | SERVING SIZE: 1 BOWL

Rimmed baking sheet lined with parchment paper or a silicone mat

3 tbsp (45 mL) olive oil or canola oil

1 tsp (5 mL) dried parsley

½ tsp (2 mL) garlic powder

¼ tsp (1 mL) salt

⅛ tsp (0.5 mL) ground black pepper

3 medium red potatoes, cut into 1-inch (2.5 cm) slices

1½ lbs (750 g) tuna, cut into 4 fillets

2 lemons, thinly sliced, divided

4 large eggs

2 cups (500 mL) fresh green beans, trimmed and halved crosswise

2 cups (500 mL) lightly packed baby spinach

1 cup (250 mL) cherry tomatoes, halved

PREHEAT THE OVEN TO 425°F (220°C).

1 In a large bowl, whisk together oil, parsley, garlic powder, salt and pepper. Add potatoes; toss to coat. Spread on the prepared baking sheet in a single layer, reserving bowl. Roast in the preheated oven for 15 minutes.

2 Meanwhile, place the tuna fillets in reserved bowl; turn to coat.

3 Remove the baking sheet from the oven, flip the potatoes and push them to the sides. Add the tuna fillets and top with half the lemon slices. Continue roasting until the potatoes are golden brown and the fish reaches an internal temperature of 145°F (63°C), about 12 minutes.

4 Meanwhile, place eggs in a medium saucepan and add enough water to cover; bring to a boil over high heat. Cook for 3 minutes, then remove from the heat, cover and let stand for 15 minutes. Drain, reserving the saucepan, and place eggs in a bowl filled with ice water until completely cool, about 10 minutes. Peel eggs and slice into quarters lengthwise.

5 Add 1 inch (2.5 cm) water to the reserved saucepan and fit with a steamer basket; bring to a boil over high heat. Add the green beans, cover and reduce the heat to medium-low; steam until tender-crisp, about 5 minutes. Transfer beans to a clean plate.

6 To each of 4 bowls, add ½ cup (125 mL) spinach and ¼ cup (60 mL) tomatoes. Top with about ⅔ cup (150 mL) potatoes and ½ cup (125 mL) green beans. Top with 1 tuna fillet and 1 sliced egg. Garnish with 1 or 2 lemon slices. Serve immediately.

NUTRITION INFORMATION (PER SERVING)	Calories: 539 • Total Fat: 24 g • Saturated Fat: 5 g
	Protein: 51 g • Total Carbohydrates: 29 g • Fiber: 5 g
	Sugars: 5 g • Sodium: 326 mg • Cholesterol: 251 mg

Toby's Tip

Swap the tuna fillets for 8 oz (250 g) drained canned tuna instead. Then you can skip the cooking and save money!

BOWLS

BRUSSELS SPROUTS, KALE AND FARRO BOWLS

This recipe is packed with everything I want from a bowl: a hearty base, tons of veggies and a nice crunchy finish.

SERVES 4 | SERVING SIZE: 1 BOWL

Rimmed baking sheet lined with parchment paper or a silicone mat

1 cup (250 mL) farro

2 cups (500 mL) water

1 cup (250 mL) low-sodium vegetable broth

1 lb (500 g) Brussels sprouts, halved

1 lb (500 g) butternut squash, cubed

3 tbsp (45 mL) olive oil, divided

2 tbsp (30 mL) liquid honey

¼ tsp + ⅛ tsp (1.5 mL) salt, divided

6 cups (1.5 L) chopped kale

2 medium carrots, shredded

⅛ tsp (0.5 mL) ground black pepper

¼ cup (60 mL) chopped walnuts

¼ cup (60 mL) crumbled goat cheese

PREHEAT THE OVEN TO 425°F (220°C).

1   In a medium saucepan, combine the farro, water and vegetable broth; bring to a boil over high heat. Reduce heat to medium-low, cover and simmer until the farro is cooked through, about 30 minutes. Fluff with a fork and set aside to cool slightly.

2   In a large bowl, combine the Brussels sprouts, squash, 2 tbsp (30 mL) olive oil, honey and ¼ tsp (1 mL) salt. Spread the mixture on the prepared baking sheet in a single layer.

3   Place the baking sheet in the preheated oven and roast the vegetables, turning halfway through, until they begin to brown, about 25 minutes. Remove the baking sheet from the oven and set aside to cool slightly, about 5 minutes.

4   In a large skillet, heat the remaining 1 tbsp (15 mL) olive oil over medium heat until shimmering. Add the kale, carrots, pepper and remaining ⅛ tsp (0.5 mL) salt; cook until the kale has wilted and carrots have softened, about 3 minutes.

5   In each of 4 bowls, arrange ½ cup (125 mL) cooked farro and 1½ cups (375 mL) roasted vegetable mixture side by side. Top with about ½ cup (125 mL) carrot-kale mixture. Sprinkle with 1 tbsp (15 mL) each of the walnuts and goat cheese. Serve warm.

NUTRITION INFORMATION (PER SERVING)	Calories: 468 • Total Fat: 19 g • Saturated Fat: 3 g
	Protein: 16 g • Total Carbohydrates: 66 g • Fiber: 14 g
	Sugars: 14 g • Sodium: 397 mg • Cholesterol: 4 mg

WARMING SWEET POTATO AND RICOTTA BOWLS

In these bowls, roasted sweet potatoes, sautéed spinach and sweet ricotta cheese come together to make the most delicious cozy dish for a cold day. I've added pumpkin seeds to give it a little crunch.

SERVES 4 | SERVING SIZE: 1 BOWL

Rimmed baking sheet lined with parchment paper or a silicone mat

2 medium sweet potatoes, peeled and cut into 1-inch (2.5 cm) cubes

½ medium red onion, thinly sliced

¼ cup (60 mL) olive oil, divided

1 tsp (5 mL) dried rosemary

½ tsp (2 mL) salt, divided

¼ tsp (1 mL) ground black pepper, divided

4 cups (1 L) lightly packed baby spinach

2 tbsp (30 mL) pumpkin seeds (pepitas)

¾ cup (175 mL) part-skim ricotta cheese

PREHEAT THE OVEN TO 425°F (220°C).

1 In a medium bowl, combine the sweet potatoes, onion, 2 tbsp (30 mL) olive oil, rosemary, ¼ tsp (1 mL) salt and ⅛ tsp (0.5 mL) pepper; toss to coat. Spread the mixture on the prepared baking sheet in a single layer. Roast the vegetables in the preheated oven, turning halfway through, until golden brown, about 25 minutes.

2 Just before serving, in a large skillet, heat the remaining 2 tbsp (30 mL) olive oil over medium heat until shimmering. Add the spinach and the remaining ¼ tsp (1 mL) salt and ⅛ tsp (0.5 mL) pepper; cook, stirring occasionally, until the spinach has wilted, about 3 minutes.

3 Into each of 4 bowls, spoon ¾ cup (175 mL) sweet potato mixture and top with ¼ cup (60 mL) cooked spinach. Scoop about 3 tbsp (45 mL) ricotta on top of each and sprinkle with about 1¾ tsp (8 mL) pumpkin seeds. Serve immediately.

Toby's Tip

Substitute chopped kale for the spinach, and butternut squash for the sweet potatoes.

NUTRITION INFORMATION (PER SERVING)

Calories: 282 • Total Fat: 20 g • Saturated Fat: 5 g
Protein: 7 g • Total Carbohydrates: 21 g • Fiber: 4 g
Sugars: 5 g • Sodium: 478 mg • Cholesterol: 23 mg

TOMATO AND WHITE BEAN QUINOA BOWLS

Quinoa and beans make my go-to meal, one that is quick and easy to whip up. I like to pair them with a refreshing combination of lemon juice and fresh tomatoes. Just add some Parmesan cheese and you've got a deliciously healthy lunch.

SERVES 4 | SERVING SIZE: 1 BOWL

½ cup (125 mL) quinoa

1 cup (250 mL) low-sodium vegetable broth

4 cups (1 L) lightly packed chopped kale

3 tbsp (45 mL) freshly squeezed lemon juice, divided

3 tbsp (45 mL) + 1 tsp (5 mL) extra-virgin olive oil, divided

½ tsp (2 mL) salt, divided

1 garlic clove, minced

½ tsp (2 mL) Italian seasoning

⅛ tsp (0.5 mL) ground black pepper

1 cup (250 mL) low-sodium canned cannellini (white kidney) beans, drained and rinsed

1 cup (250 mL) cherry tomatoes, halved

4 tsp (20 mL) grated Parmesan cheese

1 In a medium saucepan, combine the quinoa and broth; bring to a boil over high heat. Reduce the heat to medium-low, cover and simmer until the water is absorbed and the quinoa is tender, about 15 minutes. Set aside for 10 minutes, then fluff with a fork.

2 Meanwhile, in a large bowl, combine the kale, 1 tbsp (15 mL) lemon juice, 1 tsp (5 mL) olive oil and ¼ tsp (1 mL) salt. Using clean hands, massage the kale until softened, about 1 minute. Evenly divide it among 4 individual serving bowls, reserving the large bowl.

3 In the large bowl, whisk together the remaining 2 tbsp (30 mL) lemon juice, remaining 3 tbsp (45 mL) olive oil, garlic, Italian seasoning, pepper and remaining ¼ tsp (1 mL) salt. Add the beans and tomatoes; toss to coat.

4 In each of the 4 serving bowls, top the kale with about ⅓ cup (75 mL) cooked quinoa and ½ cup (125 mL) tomato-bean mixture. Sprinkle each bowl with 1 tsp (5 mL) Parmesan cheese. Serve immediately.

Toby's Tip

Mix any leftover beans into a salad or add them to cooked quinoa.

NUTRITION INFORMATION (PER SERVING)	Calories: 261 • Total Fat: 12 g • Saturated Fat: 2 g
	Protein: 10 g • Total Carbohydrates: 31 g • Fiber: 7 g
	Sugars: 3 g • Sodium: 365 mg • Cholesterol: 2 mg

FRIED RICE BOWLS
WITH BROCCOLI AND CASHEWS

One of my daughter's favorite dishes is fried rice, so when I make it, I always add more veggies and finish it off with some nuts.

SERVES 4 | SERVING SIZE: 1 BOWL

Rimmed baking sheet lined with parchment paper or a silicone mat

¾ cup (175 mL) long-grain brown rice	1 tsp (5 mL) liquid honey or agave nectar
1½ cups (375 mL) water	¼ tsp (1 mL) ground ginger
4 cups (1 L) broccoli florets	1 small onion, chopped
¼ cup (60 mL) olive oil or canola oil, divided	1 garlic clove, minced
¼ tsp (1 mL) salt	1 medium red bell pepper, chopped
⅛ tsp (0.5 mL) ground black pepper	3 large eggs, beaten
1 cup (250 mL) frozen shelled edamame	2 green onions, sliced
2 tbsp (30 mL) reduced-sodium soy sauce	¼ cup (60 mL) roughly chopped cashews

PREHEAT THE OVEN TO 400°F (200°C).

1   In a medium saucepan, bring the rice and water to a boil over high heat. Reduce the heat to medium-low, cover and simmer until tender, about 35 minutes. Set aside for 10 minutes, then fluff with a fork.

2   Meanwhile, in a large bowl, combine the broccoli, 2 tbsp (30 mL) olive oil, salt and black pepper. Spread onto the prepared baking sheet in a single layer. Roast in the preheated oven, flipping once, until browned, about 15 minutes.

3   Fill a small saucepan with water halfway to the top; bring to a boil and add the edamame. Reduce the heat to medium-low and simmer until tender, about 5 minutes. Drain and set aside.

4   In a small bowl, whisk together the soy sauce, honey and ginger.

5   In a large skillet, heat the remaining 2 tbsp (30 mL) olive oil over medium heat until shimmering. Add the onion, garlic and bell pepper; cook, stirring occasionally, until softened, about 5 minutes. Add the eggs; stir constantly until cooked, 2 to 3 minutes. Add the cooked rice and edamame; stir to combine. Add the soy sauce mixture and green onions; stir to combine.

6   In each of 4 bowls, place 1¼ cups (310 mL) rice mixture and ½ cup (125 mL) roasted broccoli. Sprinkle with 1 tbsp (15 mL) cashews. Serve immediately.

NUTRITION INFORMATION (PER SERVING)
Calories: 443 • Total Fat: 24 g • Saturated Fat: 4 g
Protein: 16 g • Total Carbohydrates: 45 g • Fiber: 5 g
Sugars: 5 g • Sodium: 448 mg • Cholesterol: 140 mg

POACHED EGG SUPERFOOD BOWLS

Eggs are a perfect protein, providing you with all your essential amino acids. There are many ways to cook up this superfood, but poached is the hands-down favorite in my house. The technique can sound intimidating, but once you get the hang of it, poached eggs are really easy to make.

SERVES 4 | SERVING SIZE: 1 BOWL

3 tbsp (45 mL) olive oil, divided

1 small onion, chopped

1 garlic clove, minced

2 medium carrots, shredded

1 tsp (5 mL) dried parsley

½ tsp (2 mL) salt, divided

¼ tsp (1 mL) ground black pepper, divided

¾ cup (175 mL) jasmine rice

1½ cups (375 mL) low-sodium vegetable broth

½ cup (125 mL) canned brown lentils, drained and rinsed

1 tsp (5 mL) white vinegar

4 large eggs

½ English cucumber, chopped

2 medium plum tomatoes, chopped

½ avocado, chopped

2 tsp (10 mL) red wine vinegar

2 cups (500 mL) baby arugula, divided

¼ cup (60 mL) crumbled goat cheese, divided

1 In a medium saucepan, heat 2 tbsp (30 mL) olive oil over medium heat until shimmering. Add the onion and garlic; cook, stirring occasionally, until the onion is translucent, about 3 minutes. Add the carrots, parsley, ¼ tsp (1 mL) salt and ⅛ tsp (0.5 mL) pepper. Cook, stirring occasionally, until the carrots have softened, about 3 minutes. Add the rice and vegetable broth; bring to a boil over high heat. Reduce the heat to medium-low, cover and simmer until the rice is tender, about 15 minutes. Set aside for 10 minutes, then fluff with a fork. Stir in the lentils.

2 Meanwhile, fill a large saucepan three-quarters full with water and bring to a boil over high heat. Add the vinegar and reduce the heat to medium-low, until simmering. Break 1 egg into a small cup and hold it near the surface of the water, then gently slide the egg into the water. Repeat with the remaining eggs. Cover the saucepan and cook for 6 minutes. Using a slotted spoon, remove the eggs and drain in a bowl lined with paper towels.

3 In a medium bowl, combine the cucumber, tomatoes and avocado. Add the remaining 1 tbsp (15 mL) olive oil, red wine vinegar and remaining ¼ tsp (1 mL) salt and ⅛ tsp (0.5 mL) pepper; toss to coat.

4 In each of 4 bowls, place ½ cup (125 mL) arugula. Over each, spoon ⅔ cup (150 mL) rice-lentil mixture and ½ cup (125 mL) cucumber mixture. Top each with 1 egg and sprinkle with 1 tbsp (15 mL) goat cheese.

NUTRITION INFORMATION (PER SERVING)

Calories: 411 • Total Fat: 21 g • Saturated Fat: 5 g

Protein: 15 g • Total Carbohydrates: 42 g • Fiber: 6 g

Sugars: 5 g • Sodium: 512 mg • Cholesterol: 190 mg

ROASTED SALMON BOWLS
WITH MIXED VEGETABLES

As a mom and a dietitian, I love that my kids enjoy salmon, since it's filled with good-for-you nutrients such as heart-healthy omega-3 fats.

SERVES 4 | SERVING SIZE: 1 BOWL

Rimmed baking sheet lined with parchment paper or a silicone mat

¾ cup (175 mL) brown basmati rice

1½ cups (375 mL) low-sodium vegetable broth

1¼ lbs (625 g) salmon, cut into 4 fillets

1 tsp (5 mL) dried thyme

½ tsp (2 mL) salt, divided

¼ tsp (1 mL) ground black pepper, divided

1 medium orange, thinly sliced

2 tbsp (30 mL) olive oil or canola oil

1 medium onion, chopped

2 garlic cloves, minced

8 oz (250 g) button mushrooms, sliced

2 medium carrots, cut into 1-inch (2.5 cm) rounds

2 cups (500 mL) broccoli florets

1 medium red pepper, cut into 1-inch (2.5 cm) slices

1 tsp (5 mL) Italian seasoning

2 cups (500 mL) lightly packed baby spinach

PREHEAT THE OVEN TO 425°F (220°C).

1   In a medium saucepan, bring the rice and vegetable broth to a boil over high heat. Reduce the heat to medium-low, cover and simmer until the rice is tender, about 35 minutes. Set aside for 10 minutes, then fluff with a fork.

2   Place the salmon on the prepared baking sheet, skin sides down. Sprinkle the flesh sides with thyme, ¼ tsp (1 mL) salt and ⅛ tsp (0.5 mL) black pepper. Top with orange slices. Bake in the preheated oven until the salmon reaches an internal temperature of 145°F (63°C), about 15 minutes.

3   Meanwhile, in a large skillet, heat the olive oil over medium heat until shimmering. Add the onion and garlic; cook, stirring occasionally, until the onion has softened, about 3 minutes. Add the mushrooms, carrots, broccoli, bell pepper, Italian seasoning and remaining ¼ tsp (1 mL) salt and ⅛ tsp (0.5 mL) black pepper; cook, stirring occasionally, until vegetables are slightly softened, about 3 minutes. Add the spinach; cook, stirring occasionally, until wilted, about 2 minutes.

4   Into each of 4 bowls, spoon ⅓ cup (75 mL) rice and top with 1¼ cups (310 mL) vegetable mixture. Top each with 1 salmon fillet. Serve immediately.

NUTRITION INFORMATION (PER SERVING)	Calories: 453 • Total Fat: 17 g • Saturated Fat: 3 g
	Protein: 35 g • Total Carbohydrates: 38 g • Fiber: 4 g
	Sugars: 5 g • Sodium: 462 mg • Cholesterol: 78 mg

FISH TACO BOWLS

When my kids are in a dinner rut, these taco bowls save the day! The crispy fish, creamy slaw and flavorful pico de gallo work beautifully together.

SERVES 4 | SERVING SIZE: 1 BOWL

SLAW

2 cups (500 mL) shredded napa cabbage

¼ tsp (1 mL) salt

1 medium carrot, shredded

2 tbsp (30 mL) chopped fresh cilantro

1 medium green onion, chopped

2 tbsp (30 mL) light mayonnaise

2 tbsp (30 mL) plain nonfat Greek yogurt

1 tbsp (15 mL) freshly squeezed lime juice

⅛ tsp (0.5 mL) ground black pepper

CRISPY FISH

2 large eggs, lightly beaten

1¼ cups (310 mL) panko bread crumbs

¾ cup (175 mL) all-purpose flour

¼ tsp (1 mL) salt

⅛ tsp (0.5 mL) ground black pepper

1 lb (500 g) cod fillets, cut into twelve 2-inch (5 cm) strips

¼ cup (60 mL) canola oil, divided

TACOS

8 corn tortillas

1 cup (250 mL) Pico de Gallo (page 188) or store-bought

1 lime, quartered

1 SLAW Place cabbage in a large bowl and sprinkle with salt. Using clean hands, massage the cabbage. Let stand for 15 minutes or up to 2 hours. Over the sink, gently squeeze the cabbage to drain any excess water. Return to the bowl and add carrot, cilantro and green onion; toss.

2 In a small bowl, whisk together mayonnaise, Greek yogurt, lime juice and pepper. Spoon over the slaw and toss to coat.

3 CRISPY FISH Place beaten eggs in a medium shallow bowl.

4 In a separate medium shallow bowl, combine the panko, flour, salt and pepper.

5 Dip each fish strip into eggs; gently shake off the excess. Then dip both sides into the panko mixture. Place on a clean plate.

6 In a large skillet, heat 2 tbsp (30 mL) canola oil over medium heat until shimmering. Add half the breaded fish and cook until internal temperature reaches 145°F (63°C), about 4 minutes per side. Using a metal spatula, transfer fish to a clean plate. Repeat with remaining 2 tbsp (30 mL) oil and breaded fish.

7 In each of 4 bowls, fold 2 tortillas. Fill each with a heaping 2 tbsp (30 mL) slaw and 2 tbsp (30 mL) Pico de Gallo. To each bowl add 3 fish strips and 1 lime wedge. Serve immediately, with any leftover pico de gallo on the side.

NUTRITION INFORMATION (PER SERVING)

Calories: 480 • Total Fat: 19 g • Saturated Fat: 2 g
Protein: 30 g • Total Carbohydrates: 49 g • Fiber: 6 g
Sugars: 5 g • Sodium: 543 mg • Cholesterol: 49 mg

FARRO AND MUSHROOM BOWLS
WITH FLOUNDER

Farro is a whole grain with a nutty texture that complements the flavor of mushrooms. Topped with light flounder, it's a healthy, delicious meal the whole family will love.

SERVES 4 | SERVING SIZE: 1 BOWL

FARRO

1 tbsp (15 mL) olive oil

1 medium onion, chopped

1 garlic clove, minced

¾ cup (175 mL) pearled farro

2 cups (500 mL) low-sodium vegetable broth

2 tbsp (30 mL) dry white wine

⅛ tsp (0.5 mL) salt

⅛ tsp (0.5 mL) ground black pepper

2 cups (500 mL) lightly packed baby spinach

2 tbsp (30 mL) grated Parmesan cheese

MUSHROOMS

1 tbsp (15 mL) unsalted butter

1 tbsp (15 mL) olive oil

10 oz (300 g) cremini mushrooms, thinly sliced

6 oz (175 g) portobello mushroom caps, thinly sliced

1 garlic clove, minced

½ tsp (2 mL) dried thyme

¼ tsp (1 mL) salt

⅛ tsp (0.5 mL) ground black pepper

FLOUNDER

1½ lbs (750 g) flounder or sole, cut into 4 fillets

⅛ tsp (0.5 mL) salt

⅛ tsp (0.5 mL) ground black pepper

2 tbsp (30 mL) unsalted butter

1 small lemon, thinly sliced

1 tsp (5 mL) dried parsley

1   **FARRO** In a large saucepan, heat the olive oil over medium heat until shimmering. Add the onion and garlic; cook, stirring occasionally, until the onion is translucent, about 2 minutes. Stir in the farro, vegetable broth, white wine, salt and pepper; bring to a boil over high heat. Reduce the heat to low, cover and simmer, stirring occasionally, until the farro is tender and the liquid absorbed, about 25 minutes. Add the spinach; cook, stirring occasionally, until wilted, about 2 minutes. Stir in the Parmesan cheese. Set aside to cool slightly.

Toby's Tip

Swap the flounder for 1¾ cups (425 mL) drained and rinsed low-sodium canned cannellini (white kidney) beans. Cook in one batch in Step 3 for 8 minutes, stirring occasionally, until warmed through.

2 **MUSHROOMS** Meanwhile, in a large skillet, heat the butter and olive oil over medium heat until the butter has melted. Add the cremini mushrooms, portobello mushrooms, garlic, thyme, salt and pepper; cook, stirring occasionally, until the mushrooms have softened, about 8 minutes. Transfer the mixture to a clean bowl, reserving the skillet, and set aside to cool slightly.

3 **FLOUNDER** Sprinkle the flounder with salt and pepper. In the reserved skillet, heat the butter over medium heat until melted. Add the lemon slices and parsley; cook, stirring occasionally, for 1 minute. Using a wooden spoon, move the lemon slices to one side of the skillet and add 2 flounder fillets. Cook, flipping halfway through, until their internal temperature reaches 145°F (63°C), about 5 to 6 minutes total. Transfer the fish to a clean plate. Repeat with the remaining fillets.

4 In each of 4 bowls, arrange $3/4$ cup (175 mL) cooked farro and $1/2$ cup (125 mL) mushrooms side by side. Top with 1 fish fillet. Distribute the lemon slices and pan juices equally among the bowls. Serve warm.

NUTRITION INFORMATION (PER SERVING)	Calories: 428 • Total Fat: 21 g • Saturated Fat: 8 g Protein: 30 g • Total Carbohydrates: 30 g • Fiber: 7 g Sugars: 4 g • Sodium: 942 mg • Cholesterol: 102 mg

COCONUT LIME RICE AND SHRIMP BOWLS

The veggies in this bowl come from the salsa: jalapeños, onion and garlic balance the sweetness of the pineapple and complement the buttery shrimp. If you want more veggies, add ¼ cup (60 mL) cooked corn to each bowl.

SERVES 4 | SERVING SIZE: 1 BOWL

1 cup (250 mL) white basmati rice

1 cup (250 mL) light coconut milk

1 cup (250 mL) water

Zest and juice of 1½ limes, divided

2 tbsp (30 mL) chopped fresh cilantro

½ tsp (2 mL) salt, divided

⅛ tsp (0.5 mL) ground black pepper

1 lb (500 g) raw shrimp (size 26/30), thawed if frozen, peeled and deveined

2 tbsp (30 mL) unsalted butter

2 garlic cloves, minced

1 green onion, chopped

2 cups (500 mL) Pineapple Salsa (page 188) or store-bought

1 In a medium saucepan, bring the rice, coconut milk and water to a boil over high heat. Reduce the heat to medium-low, cover and simmer until the rice is tender, about 15 minutes. Set aside for 10 minutes, then fluff with a fork. Stir in 2 tbsp (30 mL) lime juice, lime zest, cilantro, ¼ tsp (1 mL) salt and pepper.

2 Sprinkle the shrimp with the remaining ¼ tsp (1 mL) salt.

3 In a large skillet, heat the butter over medium heat until melted. Add the garlic and remaining 1 tbsp (15 mL) lime juice; cook, stirring constantly, until the garlic is fragrant, about 30 seconds. Add the shrimp; cook, flipping once, until opaque, about 4 minutes. Sprinkle with green onion.

4 Into each of 4 bowls, spoon ⅓ cup (75 mL) rice and top with equal amounts of shrimp. Finish each bowl with ½ cup (125 mL) Pineapple Salsa. Serve immediately.

Toby's Tip

Swap the shrimp for 1 lb (500 g) diced skinless, boneless chicken breasts. Cook for 8 minutes in Step 3.

NUTRITION INFORMATION (PER SERVING)	Calories: 286 • Total Fat: 11 g • Saturated Fat: 7 g Protein: 24 g • Total Carbohydrates: 23 g • Fiber: 1 g Sugars: 9 g • Sodium: 601 mg • Cholesterol: 198 mg

SAUTÉED CHICKEN AND VEGETABLE BOWLS
WITH COUSCOUS

Pearl couscous is not as well-known in North America as traditional couscous, but I love it as a base for bowls. The texture and flavor are more akin to pasta, but sphere-shaped. Here I combine it with chicken and tons of veggies to make a wholesome meal.

SERVES 4 | SERVING SIZE: 1 BOWL

2½ cups (625 mL) low-sodium chicken broth, divided

¾ cup (175 mL) pearl couscous

½ cup (125 mL) frozen peas

1 lb (500 g) boneless, skinless chicken breasts, cut into 1-inch (2.5 cm) pieces

½ tsp (2 mL) salt, divided

⅛ tsp (0.5 mL) ground black pepper

2 tbsp (30 mL) olive oil, divided

1 medium zucchini, sliced into 1-inch (2.5 cm) rounds

1 red bell pepper, cut into 1-inch (2.5 cm) strips

2 cups (500 mL) broccoli florets, cut into bite-size pieces

1 tsp (5 mL) ground cumin

½ tsp (2 mL) paprika

½ tsp (2 mL) garlic powder

½ tsp (2 mL) onion powder

¼ tsp (1 mL) turmeric

1 can (14.5 oz/411 g) no-salt-added diced tomatoes (with juice)

½ cup (125 mL) kalamata olives, pitted and halved

1 In a medium saucepan, combine 1½ cups (375 mL) chicken broth, couscous and peas; bring to a boil over high heat. Reduce the heat to medium-low, cover and simmer until the couscous is tender, 15 minutes. Drain any excess water, stir and set aside.

2 Sprinkle the chicken with ¼ tsp (1 mL) salt and the black pepper.

3. In a large skillet, heat 1 tbsp (15 mL) olive oil over medium heat until shimmering. Add the chicken and cook, turning every 2 minutes, until browned on all sides, about 8 minutes total. Using a slotted spoon, transfer it to a clean plate, reserving the skillet.

> *Toby's Tip*
>
> Want even more veggies? Add up to 1 cup (250 mL) sliced carrots or coarsely chopped eggplant, yellow squash or cauliflower in Step 4.

4   In the reserved skillet, heat the remaining 1 tbsp (15 mL) olive oil over medium heat until shimmering. Add the zucchini, bell pepper, broccoli, cumin, paprika, garlic powder, onion powder, turmeric and remaining $\frac{1}{4}$ tsp (1 mL) salt; cook, stirring occasionally, until the vegetables have softened, about 5 minutes. Add the cooked chicken, diced tomatoes (with juice) and remaining 1 cup (250 mL) chicken broth; bring to a boil over high heat. Reduce the heat to medium-low, cover and simmer, stirring occasionally, until the flavors combine, about 15 minutes.

5   Into each of 4 bowls, spoon $\frac{1}{2}$ cup (125 mL) couscous. Top each with $1\frac{1}{2}$ cups (375 mL) chicken-and-vegetable mixture and 2 tbsp (30 mL) olives. Serve immediately.

NUTRITION INFORMATION (PER SERVING)	Calories: 442 • Total Fat: 16 g • Saturated Fat: 6 g
	Protein: 33 g • Total Carbohydrates: 44 g • Fiber: 8 g
	Sugars: 10 g • Sodium: 559 mg • Cholesterol: 83 mg

Toby's Tip

Add up to 1 cup (250 mL) more veggies, or swap those listed in the recipe for trimmed snap peas, cauliflower florets, sliced button mushrooms or sliced carrots.

NUTRITION INFORMATION (PER SERVING)

Calories: 496 • Total Fat: 15 g • Saturated Fat: 2 g

Protein: 29 g • Total Carbohydrates: 63 g • Fiber: 3 g

Sugars: 20 g • Sodium: 460 mg • Cholesterol: 73 mg

SWEET-AND-SOUR CHICKEN BOWLS
WITH BROCCOLI AND PEPPERS

Keep this recipe tucked away for those days when you're craving Chinese takeout. By making your own version, you can control the ingredients — plus you can up the veggies as much as you like.

SERVES 4 | SERVING SIZE: 1 BOWL

1 cup (250 mL) long-grain brown rice

2 cups (500 mL) water

½ cup (125 mL) 100% pineapple juice

¼ cup (60 mL) ketchup

3 tbsp (45 mL) pure maple syrup

2 tbsp (30 mL) rice wine vinegar

1 tbsp (15 mL) reduced-sodium soy sauce

¼ cup (60 mL) warm water

2 tbsp (30 mL) cornstarch

3 tbsp (45 mL) canola oil or olive oil, divided

1 lb (500 g) skinless, boneless chicken breasts, cut into 1-inch (2.5 cm) pieces

1 medium yellow bell pepper, cut into 1-inch (2.5 cm) strips

1 medium green bell pepper, cut into 1-inch (2.5 cm) strips

2 cups (500 mL) broccoli florets

2 medium green onions, chopped

1   In a medium saucepan, bring the rice and 2 cups (500 mL) water to a boil over high heat. Reduce the heat to low, cover and simmer until the rice is tender, about 35 minutes. Set aside for 10 minutes, then fluff with a fork.

2   In a medium bowl, whisk together the pineapple juice, ketchup, maple syrup, rice vinegar and soy sauce.

3   In a small bowl, whisk together the ¼ cup (60 mL) warm water and cornstarch.

4   In a large skillet, heat 2 tbsp (30 mL) canola oil over medium heat until shimmering. Add the chicken and cook, turning every 2 minutes, until browned on all sides, about 8 minutes total. Using a slotted spoon, transfer it to a clean plate, reserving the skillet.

5   In the reserved skillet, heat the remaining 1 tbsp (15 mL) canola oil over medium heat until shimmering. Add the yellow bell pepper, green bell pepper and broccoli; cook, stirring occasionally, until the vegetables have softened slightly, about 3 minutes. Add the pineapple juice mixture; raise the heat to high and cook, stirring occasionally, until beginning to bubble, about 2 minutes. Reduce the heat to medium-low and stir in the cornstarch mixture; cook, stirring constantly, until thickened slightly, about 2 minutes. Add the cooked chicken and toss to coat.

6   In each of 4 bowls, arrange ½ cup (125 mL) rice and 1¼ cups (310 mL) chicken mixture side by side. Sprinkle each bowl with an equal amount of green onion. Serve immediately.

CHICKEN AND STEAMED VEGGIE BOWLS
WITH PEANUT SAUCE

These bowls contain smooth rice noodles, tender-crisp vegetables and tasty chicken pieces, all piled high and drizzled with a peanutty sauce that brings the ingredients together beautifully.

SERVES 4 | SERVING SIZE: 1 BOWL

CHICKEN

2 tbsp (30 mL) reduced-sodium soy sauce

2 tbsp (30 mL) rice wine vinegar

2 tbsp (30 mL) canola oil, divided

1 tbsp (15 mL) freshly squeezed lime juice

1 tsp (5 mL) Sriracha

½ tsp (2 mL) liquid honey

1 lb (500 g) boneless, skinless chicken breasts, cut into 1-inch (2.5 cm) pieces

NOODLES

8 oz (250 g) dried brown udon rice noodles or soba noodles

STEAMED VEGETABLES

2 cups (500 mL) broccoli florets

2 cups (500 mL) cauliflower florets

1 medium carrot, cut into 1-inch (2.5 cm) rounds

PEANUT SAUCE

½ cup (125 mL) creamy peanut butter

6 tbsp (90 mL) warm water

2 tbsp (30 mL) reduced-sodium soy sauce

1 tbsp (15 mL) freshly squeezed lime juice

2 tsp (10 mL) liquid honey

1 tsp (5 mL) Sriracha

1 garlic clove, minced

1 **CHICKEN** In a medium bowl, whisk together the soy sauce, rice vinegar, 1 tbsp (15 mL) canola oil, lime juice, sriracha and honey. Add the chicken and toss to coat. Cover the bowl and place in the refrigerator for 20 minutes or up to 24 hours.

2 In a large skillet, heat the remaining 1 tbsp (15 mL) canola oil over medium heat until shimmering. Add the chicken and cook, turning every 2 minutes, until browned on all sides, about 8 minutes total. Using a slotted spoon, transfer the chicken to a clean plate.

3 **NOODLES** Meanwhile, fill a medium saucepan three-quarters full with water and bring to a boil over high heat. Add the udon noodles and cook according to the package directions. Drain and rinse under cool water. Set aside to cool slightly.

> *Toby's Tip*
>
> Steaming is a quick, healthy cooking method that helps maintain the nutrients in the food you're preparing.

4 **STEAMED VEGETABLES** Meanwhile, add 1 inch (2.5 cm) water to a large saucepan fitted with a steamer basket; bring the water to a boil over high heat. Place the broccoli, cauliflower and carrot in the steamer basket; cover and steam until fork-tender, about 6 minutes. Using a slotted spoon, transfer the vegetables to a clean plate.

5 **PEANUT SAUCE** In a medium bowl, whisk together the peanut butter and warm water. Add the soy sauce, lime juice, honey, Sriracha and garlic; stir. The sauce should be thick but pourable; if it is too thick for your liking, whisk in 1 to 2 tbsp (15 to 30 mL) warm water.

6 In each of 4 bowls, place ¾ cup (175 mL) udon noodles. Top with 1 cup (250 mL) steamed vegetables and ½ cup (125 mL) cooked chicken. Drizzle with about ¼ cup (60 mL) peanut sauce.

NUTRITION INFORMATION (PER SERVING)	Calories: 605 • Total Fat: 22 g • Saturated Fat: 4 g Protein: 39 g • Total Carbohydrates: 67 g • Fiber: 5 g Sugars: 9 g • Sodium: 654 mg • Cholesterol: 83 mg

CURRIED CHICKEN BOWLS
WITH SWEET POTATO AND RED PEPPER

This delectable bowl will fill your home with the most wonderful scent of warming spices. It's a hearty dish that freezes beautifully!

SERVES 4 | SERVING SIZE: 1 BOWL

1½ cups (375 mL) low-sodium chicken broth, divided

½ cup (125 mL) quinoa

1 lb (500 g) skinless, boneless chicken tenders

½ tsp (2 mL) salt, divided

⅛ tsp (0.5 mL) ground black pepper

2 tbsp (30 mL) canola oil, divided

1 medium onion, diced

1 garlic clove, minced

1 red bell pepper, diced

2 medium sweet potatoes, peeled and cut into 1-inch (2.5 cm) pieces

1½ cups (375 mL) light coconut milk

1 can (14.5 oz/411 g) no-salt-added diced tomatoes (with juice)

2 tbsp (30 mL) tomato paste

4 tsp (20 mL) curry powder

⅛ tsp (0.5 mL) ground cloves

1 In a medium saucepan, bring 1 cup (250 mL) broth and quinoa to a boil over high heat. Reduce heat to medium-low, cover and simmer until quinoa is tender, about 15 minutes. Set aside for 10 minutes, then fluff with a fork.

2 Sprinkle both sides of the chicken with ¼ tsp (1 mL) salt and black pepper.

3 In a large high-sided skillet, heat 1 tbsp (15 mL) canola oil over medium heat until shimmering. Add chicken and cook, turning once, until browned on both sides, about 6 minutes total. Using a slotted spoon, transfer chicken to a clean plate, reserving the pan.

4 In the reserved sauté pan, heat remaining 1 tbsp (15 mL) canola oil over medium heat until shimmering. Add onion and garlic; cook, stirring occasionally, until the onion is translucent, about 3 minutes. Add the bell pepper; cook, stirring occasionally, until softened, about 3 minutes. Add sweet potatoes, remaining ½ cup (125 mL) broth, coconut milk, diced tomatoes (with juice), tomato paste, curry powder, cloves, remaining ¼ tsp (1 mL) salt and cooked chicken; stir and bring the mixture to a boil over high heat. Reduce heat to medium-low, cover and simmer, stirring occasionally, until sweet potatoes have softened and flavors combine, about 20 minutes.

5 Spoon ½ cup (125 mL) quinoa into each of 4 bowls; top with 1¾ cups (425 mL) curried chicken mixture. Evenly distribute any sauce remaining at the bottom of the pan. Serve warm.

NUTRITION INFORMATION (PER SERVING)	Calories: 453 • Total Fat: 18 g • Saturated Fat: 2 g
	Protein: 33 g • Total Carbohydrates: 41 g • Fiber: 6 g
	Sugars: 8 g • Sodium: 814 mg • Cholesterol: 83 mg

UNSTUFFED PEPPER BOWLS

When I was a girl, my grandma made the best stuffed peppers. This version takes the main components of that dish — beef, rice and tomatoes — and puts them together in a healthier bowl, using lean beef, brown rice and even more veggies, of course!

SERVES 4 | SERVING SIZE: 1 BOWL

1 cup (250 mL) brown basmati rice

2 cups (500 mL) low-sodium beef broth

2 tbsp (30 mL) olive oil, divided

1 lb (500 g) ground beef, at least 90% lean

1 medium onion, chopped

2 garlic cloves, minced

8 oz (250 g) button mushrooms, thinly sliced

1 red bell pepper, cut into 1-inch (2.5 cm) strips

1 green bell pepper, cut into 1-inch (2.5 cm) strips

1 can (14.5 oz/411 g) no-salt-added diced tomatoes (with juice)

½ cup (125 mL) prepared tomato sauce

1 tsp (5 mL) dried parsley

½ tsp (2 mL) dried thyme

½ tsp (2 mL) dried basil

¼ tsp (1 mL) salt

⅛ tsp (0.5 mL) ground black pepper

½ cup (125 mL) shredded reduced-fat Cheddar cheese

1   Place the rice and beef broth in a medium saucepan; bring to a boil over high heat. Reduce the heat to medium-low, cover and simmer until the rice is tender, 35 minutes. Set aside for 10 minutes, then fluff with a fork.

2   Meanwhile, in a large skillet, heat 1 tbsp (15 mL) olive oil over medium heat until shimmering. Add the beef; cook, stirring occasionally, until browned, about 8 minutes. Using a slotted spoon, transfer the meat to a clean bowl, reserving the skillet.

3   In the reserved skillet, heat the remaining 1 tbsp (15 mL) olive oil over medium heat until shimmering. Add the onion and garlic; cook, stirring occasionally, until the onion is translucent, about 3 minutes. Add the mushrooms, red bell pepper and green bell pepper; cook, stirring occasionally, until the peppers have softened slightly, about 5 minutes. Add the cooked ground beef, diced tomatoes (with juice), tomato sauce, parsley, thyme, basil, salt and black pepper; stir to combine. Bring the mixture to a boil over high heat, then reduce the heat to medium-low, cover and simmer until the flavors combine, about 15 minutes.

4   Into each of 4 bowls, spoon ½ cup (125 mL) cooked rice, top with 1¾ cups (425 mL) ground beef mixture and sprinkle with 2 tbsp (30 mL) Cheddar cheese. Serve warm.

NUTRITION INFORMATION (PER SERVING)

Calories: 534 • Total Fat: 24 g • Saturated Fat: 4 g
Protein: 27 g • Total Carbohydrates: 56 g • Fiber: 9 g
Sugars: 5 g • Sodium: 657 mg • Cholesterol: 53 mg

FLANK STEAK BOWLS
WITH BLACK BEANS, PEPPERS AND ONIONS

There's no need to eat out when you can make your own spin on fajitas for a fraction of the cost!

SERVES 4 | SERVING SIZE: 1 BOWL

⅓ cup (75 mL) olive oil, divided

½ tsp (2 mL) garlic powder

½ tsp (2 mL) onion powder

½ tsp (2 mL) salt, divided

¼ tsp (1 mL) ground black pepper, divided

12 oz (375 g) flank steak

1 cup (250 mL) long-grain brown rice

2 cups (500 mL) water

1 cup (250 mL) low-sodium canned black beans, drained and rinsed

1 garlic clove, minced

1 medium onion, thinly sliced

1 medium red bell pepper, cut into 1-inch (2.5 cm) strips

1 medium green bell pepper, cut into 1-inch (2.5 cm) strips

1 tsp (5 mL) dried oregano

½ cup (125 mL) prepared tomato salsa

1 In a medium bowl, whisk together 2 tbsp (30 mL) olive oil, garlic powder, onion powder, ¼ tsp (1 mL) salt and ⅛ tsp (0.5 mL) black pepper.

2 Cut the steak in half lengthwise, then cut it crosswise into slices ¼ inch (0.5 cm) thick. Place in the bowl with the olive oil mixture; toss to coat. Cover and refrigerate for at least 20 minutes or up to 24 hours.

3 Place the rice and water in a medium saucepan; bring to a boil over high heat. Reduce the heat to medium-low, cover and simmer until the rice is tender, about 40 minutes. Set aside for 10 minutes, then fluff with a fork. Stir in the black beans.

4 In a large skillet, heat 2 tbsp (30 mL) olive oil over medium heat until shimmering. Add the garlic and cook until fragrant, about 30 seconds. Add the onion, red bell pepper, green bell pepper, oregano and remaining ¼ tsp (1 mL) salt and ⅛ tsp (0.5 mL) black pepper; cook, stirring occasionally, until the vegetables have softened, about 7 minutes. Transfer to a plate, reserving the skillet.

5 In the skillet, heat the remaining 1 tbsp (15 mL) olive oil over medium-high heat until shimmering. In batches as necessary, remove the steak from the bowl, allowing excess marinade to drip off, and add to the skillet. Cook until the meat is browned and reaches an internal temperature of 145°F (63°C), about 3 minutes on each side.

6 Into each of 4 bowls, spoon 1 cup (250 mL) rice-and-bean mixture and gently push it down with the back of the spoon. Arrange ⅔ cup (150 mL) vegetables beside the rice. Top with about 3 oz (90 g) steak and 2 tbsp (30 mL) salsa.

JERK-SEASONED PORK BOWLS
WITH SWEET POTATO AND PINEAPPLE

I love making these bowls when I want to feel like I'm somewhere hot on a cold day. If you're short on time, omit the avocado and cilantro from the salsa.

SERVES 4 | SERVING SIZE: 1 BOWL

Rimmed baking sheet lined with parchment paper or a silicone mat

1 cup (250 mL) water	½ tsp (2 mL) ground cinnamon
1 cup (250 mL) light coconut milk	½ tsp (2 mL) salt
1 cup (250 mL) jasmine rice	½ tsp (2 mL) granulated sugar
¼ cup (60 mL) canola oil	¼ tsp (1 mL) ground nutmeg
2 tsp (10 mL) garlic powder	4 boneless pork chops, each 4 oz (125 g)
1 tsp (5 mL) onion powder	2 medium sweet potatoes, peeled and cut into 1-inch (2.5 cm) pieces
1 tsp (5 mL) dried parsley	
1 tsp (5 mL) ground allspice	1 avocado, diced
½ tsp (2 mL) cayenne pepper	1 cup (250 mL) fresh or canned pineapple in its own juice, diced
½ tsp (2 mL) dried thyme	2 tbsp (30 mL) chopped fresh cilantro

PREHEAT THE OVEN TO 400°F (200°C).

1   In a medium saucepan, combine the water, coconut milk and rice; bring to a boil over high heat. Reduce the heat to medium-low, cover and simmer until the rice is tender, about 15 minutes. Set aside for 10 minutes, then fluff with a fork.

2   Meanwhile, in a large shallow bowl, combine the canola oil, garlic powder, onion powder, parsley, allspice, cayenne pepper, thyme, cinnamon, salt, sugar and nutmeg. Transfer half this marinade to a separate large bowl.

3   Add the pork chops to the shallow bowl; turn to coat. Remove the chops, shaking off the excess, and place on a clean plate.

4   Add the sweet potatoes to the large bowl; toss to coat. Spread on the prepared baking sheet in a single layer. Bake in the preheated oven until they are starting to brown, 15 minutes. Remove the baking sheet from the oven, push the sweet potatoes to the sides of the sheet, maintaining a single layer, and place the pork chops in the center. Bake, turning the pork chops halfway through, until the sweet potatoes have browned and the internal temperature of the chops reaches 145°F (63°C), about 8 minutes.

5   Meanwhile, in a medium bowl, combine the avocado, pineapple and cilantro.

6   Into each of 4 bowls, spoon ½ cup (125 mL) cooked rice; add ⅔ cup (150 mL) sweet potato and 1 pork chop. Top with ⅓ cup (75 mL) pineapple salsa. Serve immediately.

NUTRITION INFORMATION (PER SERVING)

Calories: 625 • Total Fat: 29 g • Saturated Fat: 7 g
Protein: 31 g • Total Carbohydrates: 64 g • Fiber: 6 g
Sugars: 8 g • Sodium: 610 mg • Cholesterol: 54 mg

CAJUN-FLAVORED VEGETABLE AND ANDOUILLE SAUSAGE BOWLS

These bowls are perfect for a quick and easy family-night dinner, and you can take any leftovers to work to heat and eat. If you can't find andouille sausage, any spicy smoked sausage or dried chorizo will work just fine.

SERVES 4 | SERVING SIZE: 1 BOWL

Rimmed baking sheet lined with parchment paper or a silicone mat

2 red bell peppers, cut into 1-inch (2.5 cm) strips

2 cups (500 mL) Brussels sprouts, halved

2 cups (500 mL) broccoli florets

3 tbsp (45 mL) olive oil

2 tsp (10 mL) Cajun seasoning

1/2 tsp (2 mL) garlic powder

1/4 tsp (1 mL) salt

12 oz (375 oz) andouille sausage, sliced into 1-inch (2.5 cm) rounds

2 cups (500 mL) water

1/2 cup (125 mL) yellow cornmeal or polenta

1 tbsp (15 mL) unsalted butter

2 tbsp (30 mL) grated Parmesan cheese

PREHEAT THE OVEN TO 400°F (200°C).

1 In a large bowl, combine the bell peppers, Brussels sprouts, broccoli florets, olive oil, Cajun seasoning, garlic powder and salt; toss to coat. Spoon the vegetables onto the prepared baking sheet in a single layer.

2 Bake in the preheated oven for 12 minutes. Remove from the oven; stir the vegetables and add the sausage. Continue baking until the vegetables have browned and the sausage is heated through, about 10 more minutes.

3 In a medium saucepan, bring the water to a boil over high heat. Reduce the heat to low and, stirring constantly, slowly whisk in the cornmeal. Cook, stirring frequently, until polenta has thickened, 10 to 12 minutes. Remove from the heat and add the butter and Parmesan cheese; stir frequently until the butter has melted.

4 Into each of 4 bowls, spoon 1/2 cup (125 mL) polenta. Top with 1 1/2 cups (375 mL) sausage-and-vegetable mixture. Serve immediately.

Toby's Tip

You can find andouille sausage — a smoked sausage made from pork — in the deli section of your supermarket or next to cured meats such as bacon.

NUTRITION INFORMATION (PER SERVING)

Calories: 447 • Total Fat: 31 g • Saturated Fat: 8 g
Protein: 19 g • Total Carbohydrates: 25 g • Fiber: 4 g
Sugars: 4 g • Sodium: 1,454 mg • Cholesterol: 72 mg

CHAPTER 9

TOPPERS AND ACCOMPANIMENTS

PARMESAN CROUTONS

These crunchy croutons are made with whole-grain bread and flavored with delicious, umami-flavored cheese.

MAKES 6 SERVINGS (3 CUPS/750 ML)
SERVING SIZE: ½ CUP (125 ML)

Rimmed baking sheet lined with parchment paper or a silicone mat

¼ cup (60 mL) olive oil

¼ cup (60 mL) grated Parmesan cheese

1 tsp (5 mL) garlic powder

¼ tsp (1 mL) salt

⅛ tsp (0.5 mL) ground black pepper

4 slices 100% whole wheat bread, cut into 1-inch (2.5 cm) pieces

PREHEAT THE OVEN TO 400°F (200°C).

1 In a medium bowl, whisk together the olive oil, Parmesan cheese, garlic powder, salt and pepper. Add the bread and toss until the oil is soaked up.

2 Spread the bread pieces on the prepared baking sheet in a single layer. Bake in the preheated oven, tossing halfway through, until browned and crisp, about 10 minutes.

3 Remove the baking sheet from the oven and let cool for at least 10 minutes or up to 30 minutes. Using a spatula, break up any pieces that have stuck together.

NUTRITION INFORMATION (PER SERVING)

Calories: 146
Total Fat: 11 g • Saturated Fat: 2 g
Protein: 4 g • Total Carbohydrates: 8 g
Fiber: 1 g • Sugars: 1 g
Sodium: 237 mg • Cholesterol: 4 mg

PARMESAN CRISPS

These crisps add the perfect low-carb crunch to crumble and sprinkle over a soup, salad or bowl. Try them with Broccoli Cheddar Soup (page 82) or Caesar Salad with Grilled Cod (page 134). Or serve them whole, alongside a sandwich.

MAKES 4 SERVINGS (8 CRISPS)
SERVING SIZE: 2 CRISPS

Rimmed baking sheet lined with parchment paper

½ cup (125 mL) grated Parmesan cheese

⅛ tsp (0.5 mL) ground black pepper

PREHEAT THE OVEN TO 400°F (200°C).

1 In a medium bowl, combine the Parmesan cheese and pepper.

2 Create 8 piles, approximately 1 tbsp (15 mL) each, of cheese mixture on the prepared baking sheet, spacing at least ½ inch (1 cm) apart.

3 Bake in the preheated oven until crispy and golden brown, about 5 minutes.

4 Let the crisps cool completely. Using a spatula, transfer to a clean plate. Serve immediately or store in an airtight container at room temperature for up to 5 days.

TOBY'S TIP: Swap the Parmesan cheese for asiago or Cheddar cheese.

NUTRITION INFORMATION (PER SERVING)

Calories: 54
Total Fat: 4 g • Saturated Fat: 2 g
Protein: 5 g • Total Carbohydrates: 1 g
Fiber: 0 g • Sugars: 0 g
Sodium: 191 mg • Cholesterol: 11 mg

PESTO

This gorgeous green sauce makes a wonderful topper for fish, chicken and even soups and bowls. It works great in Roasted Carrot Soup with Pesto (page 79).

MAKES 8 SERVINGS (½ CUP/125 ML)
SERVING SIZE: 1 TBSP (15 ML)

Food processor

¼ cup (60 mL) pine nuts

2 tbsp (30 mL) shredded Romano cheese

2 tbsp (30 mL) freshly squeezed lemon juice

1 garlic clove, crushed

¼ tsp (1 mL) salt

⅛ tsp (0.5 mL) ground black pepper

2 cups (500 mL) packed fresh basil leaves

6 tbsp (90 mL) extra-virgin olive oil

1 In a food processor, combine the pine nuts, Romano cheese, lemon juice, garlic, salt and pepper; pulse until finely ground. Add the basil; pulse until incorporated. With the motor running, slowly drizzle in the olive oil; pulse until a smooth paste forms.

2 Serve immediately or store in an airtight container in the refrigerator for up to 1 week.

TOBY'S TIP: If you prefer, use walnuts instead of pine nuts.

NUTRITION INFORMATION (PER SERVING)

Calories: 151
Total Fat: 15 g • Saturated Fat: 2 g
Protein: 3 g • Total Carbohydrates: 5 g
Fiber: 3 g • Sugars: 0 g
Sodium: 109 mg • Cholesterol: 1 mg

SPICY ROASTED RED PEPPER HUMMUS

Do you want to add creaminess and spice to your salads, or perhaps try something new as a mayo replacement? This hummus can do both!

MAKES 14 SERVINGS
(1¾ CUPS/425 ML)
SERVING SIZE: 2 TBSP (30 ML)

Blender

1⅔ cups (400 mL) low-sodium canned chickpeas, drained and rinsed

⅓ cup (75 mL) jarred roasted red peppers, with liquid

1 jalapeño pepper, seeded and roughly chopped

1 garlic clove, crushed

2 tbsp (30 mL) freshly squeezed lemon juice

1 tbsp (15 mL) tahini

¼ tsp (1 mL) salt

¼ cup (60 mL) extra-virgin olive oil

1 In a blender, combine the chickpeas, roasted red peppers, jalapeño, garlic, lemon juice, tahini and salt; blend on high speed until smooth, about 1 minute. With the motor running on low speed, slowly drizzle in the olive oil; blend until combined.

2 Serve immediately or store in an airtight container in the refrigerator for up to 5 days.

NUTRITION INFORMATION (PER SERVING)

Calories: 70
Total Fat: 5 g • Saturated Fat: 1 g
Protein: 2 g • Total Carbohydrates: 5 g
Fiber: 1 g • Sugars: 1 g
Sodium: 138 mg • Cholesterol: 0 mg

PINEAPPLE SALSA

This sweet salsa tastes great with fish. I use it in Coconut Lime Rice and Shrimp Bowls (page 167) and Fish Taco Bowls (page 162).

MAKES 4 SERVINGS (2 CUPS/500 ML)
SERVING SIZE: ½ CUP (125 ML)

1 cup (250 mL) fresh or canned pineapple in its own juices, diced

½ red bell pepper, diced

¼ small red onion, diced

½ jalapeño pepper, seeded and finely chopped

¼ cup (60 mL) chopped fresh cilantro

2 tbsp (30 mL) freshly squeezed lime juice

¼ tsp (1 mL) salt

1   In a medium bowl, combine the pineapple, bell pepper, onion, jalapeño, cilantro, lime juice and salt. Cover and refrigerate for at least 20 minutes or up to 24 hours to allow the flavors to combine.

TOBY'S TIP: If you're using fresh pineapple, cut it all up and then store the remaining amount in an airtight container in the refrigerator for up to 4 days, to enjoy as a snack or dessert.

NUTRITION INFORMATION (PER SERVING)

Calories: 3
Total Fat: 0 g • Saturated Fat: 0 g
Protein: 0 g • Total Carbohydrates: 10 g
Fiber: 1 g • Sugars: 8 g
Sodium: 154 mg • Cholesterol: 0 mg

PICO DE GALLO

Pico de gallo is a fresh salsa that's typically used with Mexican-inspired dishes. It tends to be chunkier and has less liquid than tomato salsas that contain cooked ingredients. Try it with Fish Taco Bowls (page 162).

MAKES 8 SERVINGS (2 CUPS/500 ML)
SERVING SIZE: ¼ CUP (60 ML)

3 plum tomatoes, diced

½ medium white onion, diced

½ jalapeño pepper, seeded and finely diced

2 garlic cloves, minced

2 tbsp (30 mL) freshly squeezed lime juice

2 tbsp (30 mL) chopped fresh cilantro

¼ tsp (1 mL) salt

1   In a small bowl, combine the tomatoes, onion, jalapeño, garlic, lime juice, cilantro and salt. Serve immediately or cover and store in the refrigerator for up to 4 days.

TOBY'S TIP: White onions have a sharper flavor than yellow onions and are also more tender, with a thinner skin.

NUTRITION INFORMATION (PER SERVING)

Calories: 9
Total Fat: 0 g • Saturated Fat: 0 g
Protein: 0 g • Total Carbohydrates: 2 g
Fiber: 0 g • Sugars: 1 g
Sodium: 75 mg • Cholesterol: 0 mg

CRUSTY HERBED BREAD

There's nothing more satisfying than crunchy, flavorful slices of bread to accompany salads or dip into soups. I especially like this alongside Broccoli Cheddar Soup (page 82) or Kale and Sweet Potato Salad with Shredded Chicken (page 138).

MAKES 10 SERVINGS (30 SLICES)
SERVING SIZE: 3 SLICES

Rimmed baking sheet lined with parchment paper or a silicone mat

¼ cup (60 mL) olive oil

2 tbsp (30 mL) unsalted butter, softened

2 garlic cloves, minced

1 tbsp (15 mL) grated Parmesan cheese

1 tbsp (15 mL) Italian seasoning

1 French baguette (10 oz/300 g), cut into thirty 1-inch (2.5 cm) slices

PREHEAT THE OVEN TO 425°F (220°C).

1 In a medium bowl, whisk together the olive oil, butter, garlic, Parmesan cheese and Italian seasoning.

2 Lay the bread slices on the prepared baking sheet in a single layer. Brush the top of each slice with the oil mixture. Bake in the preheated oven until the tops are crispy and slightly browned, about 8 minutes. Serve warm.

NUTRITION INFORMATION (PER SERVING)

Calories: 124
Total Fat: 6 g • Saturated Fat: 2 g
Protein: 3 g • Total Carbohydrates: 14 g
Fiber: 2 g • Sugars: 1 g
Sodium: 168 mg • Cholesterol: 5 mg

WHOLE WHEAT PITA CHIPS

Next time you feel like reaching for a bag of pita chips, try making them at home instead. They are super quick to prepare and delicious crumbled over salads and soups or served on the side. These pair well with Chickpea Salad with Couscous (page 124) and Speedy Vegetable Soup (page 85).

MAKES 12 SERVINGS (24 CHIPS)
SERVING SIZE: 2 CHIPS

2 rimmed baking sheets lined with parchment paper or silicone mats

½ cup (125 mL) olive oil

½ tsp (2 mL) kosher salt

¼ tsp (1 mL) ground black pepper

Four 6½-inch (17 cm) whole wheat pitas, each cut into 6 triangles

PREHEAT THE OVEN TO 375°F (190°C).

1 In a large bowl, whisk together the olive oil, salt and pepper.

2 Lay the pita triangles in single layers on the prepared baking sheets. Brush both sides of the pita with the oil mixture. Bake in the preheated oven, turning the triangles halfway through, until crispy, about 12 minutes. Serve immediately or store at room temperature for up to 1 week.

NUTRITION INFORMATION (PER SERVING)

Calories: 106
Total Fat: 7 g • Saturated Fat: 1 g
Protein: 2 g • Total Carbohydrates: 9 g
Fiber: 2 g • Sugars: 1 g
Sodium: 170 mg • Cholesterol: 0 mg

CRUNCHY CHICKPEAS

These crunchy chickpeas are perfect to top salads or soups, like Greek Salad with Edamame (page 125) or Broccoli Cheddar Soup (page 82).

MAKES 6 SERVINGS (1½ CUPS/375 ML)
SERVING SIZE: ABOUT ¼ CUP (60 ML)

Rimmed baking sheet lined with parchment paper or a silicone mat

3½ cups (875 mL) low-sodium canned chickpeas, drained, rinsed and patted dry

2 tbsp (30 mL) olive oil

1 tbsp (15 mL) Italian seasoning

½ tsp (2 mL) kosher salt

¼ tsp (1 mL) ground black pepper

PREHEAT THE OVEN TO 375°F (190°C).

1   Remove any loose skins from the chickpeas.

2   Spread the chickpeas on the prepared baking sheet in a single layer. Drizzle with the oil and sprinkle with Italian seasoning, salt and pepper. Gently shake the baking sheet to evenly distribute the oil and spices.

3   Bake in the preheated oven, gently stirring every 5 minutes, until the chickpeas are crispy, about 50 minutes. Let cool completely before transferring to a serving bowl.

NUTRITION INFORMATION (PER SERVING)

Calories: 164
Total Fat: 7 g • Saturated Fat: 1 g
Protein: 7 g • Total Carbohydrates: 19 g
Fiber: 6 g • Sugars: 4 g
Sodium: 364 mg • Cholesterol: 0 mg

CARAMELIZED ONIONS

When onions are cooked over low heat for a long time, the sugar in them caramelizes, giving the dishes they are added to a rich and savory flavor. Try adding them to the Lentil Salad with Chopped Vegetables (page 127).

MAKES 4 SERVINGS (1 CUP/250 ML)
SERVING SIZE: ¼ CUP (60 ML)

1 tbsp (15 mL) unsalted butter

1 tbsp (15 mL) canola oil or olive oil

2 medium onions, cut into 1-inch (2.5 cm) slices

¼ tsp (1 mL) salt

1   In a medium skillet, heat the butter and canola oil over medium heat until the butter has melted. Add the onions and salt; reduce the heat to medium-low and cook, stirring every 2 minutes, until the onions are browned, about 40 minutes. If the onions start to stick to the pan, add 1 tbsp (15 mL) water; using a wooden spoon, scrape the bottom of the skillet, repeating as necessary.

2   Transfer the onions to a clean bowl. Serve warm.

TOBY'S TIP: You can store whole onions in a cool, dry, dark place (such as the back of your pantry) for up to 8 weeks.

NUTRITION INFORMATION (PER SERVING)

Calories: 70
Total Fat: 5 g • Saturated Fat: 1 g
Protein: 1 g • Total Carbohydrates: 5 g
Fiber: 1 g • Sugars: 2 g
Sodium: 151 mg • Cholesterol: 4 mg

CHAPTER 10

DRESSINGS

BALSAMIC VINAIGRETTE

This basic dressing takes 10 minutes to whip up. It's great on Greek Salad with Edamame (page 125) and can be used instead of the Red Wine Vinaigrette on the Lentil Salad with Chopped Vegetables (page 127).

MAKES 4 SERVINGS (½ CUP/125 ML)
SERVING SIZE: 2 TBSP (30 ML)

¼ cup (60 mL) balsamic vinegar

1 tsp (5 mL) liquid honey or agave nectar

1 tsp (5 mL) Dijon mustard

½ tsp (2 mL) onion powder

½ tsp (2 mL) garlic powder

½ tsp (2 mL) dried rosemary

¼ tsp (1 mL) salt

⅛ tsp (0.5 mL) ground black pepper

¼ cup (60 mL) extra-virgin olive oil

1   In a small bowl, whisk together the balsamic vinegar, honey, mustard, onion powder, garlic powder, rosemary, salt and pepper. Slowly drizzle in the olive oil, whisking constantly until incorporated.

2   Use immediately or cover and refrigerate for up to 1 week.

NUTRITION INFORMATION (PER SERVING)

Calories: 140
Total Fat: 14 g • Saturated Fat: 2 g
Protein: 0 g • Total Carbohydrates: 4 g
Fiber: 0 g • Sugars: 3 g
Sodium: 178 mg • Cholesterol: 0 mg

RED WINE VINAIGRETTE

You can make this versatile vinaigrette in less than 10 minutes. Use it over salads or as a marinade for chicken, fish or tofu (simply marinate your protein for a minimum of 30 minutes or up to 4 hours).

MAKES 6 SERVINGS (¾ CUP/175 ML)
SERVING SIZE: 2 TBSP (30 ML)

¼ cup (60 mL) red wine vinegar

1 tbsp (15 mL) Dijon mustard

1 tsp (5 mL) agave nectar

1 tsp (5 mL) Italian seasoning

¼ tsp (1 mL) garlic powder

¼ tsp (1 mL) salt

½ cup (125 mL) extra-virgin olive oil

1   In a small bowl, whisk together the red wine vinegar, mustard, agave nectar, Italian seasoning, garlic powder and salt. Slowly drizzle in the olive oil, whisking constantly until incorporated.

2   Use immediately or cover and refrigerate for up to 1 week.

TOBY'S TIP: Use this dressing on the Chickpea Salad with Couscous (page 124).

NUTRITION INFORMATION (PER SERVING)

Calories: 169
Total Fat: 19 g • Saturated Fat: 3 g
Protein: 0 g • Total Carbohydrates: 2 g
Fiber: 0 g • Sugars: 1 g
Sodium: 160 mg • Cholesterol: 0 mg

LEMON VINAIGRETTE

This refreshing vinaigrette is my go-to salad dressing because it complements pretty much any green salad.

MAKES 6 SERVINGS (¾ CUP/175 ML)
SERVING SIZE: 2 TBSP (30 ML)

¼ cup (60 mL) apple cider vinegar

Zest and juice of 1 lemon

2 tsp (10 mL) Dijon mustard

1 garlic clove, minced

1 tsp (5 mL) dried oregano

1 tsp (5 mL) dried parsley

¼ tsp (1 mL) salt

⅛ tsp (0.5 mL) ground black pepper

½ cup (125 mL) extra-virgin olive oil

1 In a medium bowl, whisk together the apple cider vinegar, lemon zest, lemon juice mustard, garlic, oregano, parsley, salt and pepper. Slowly drizzle in the olive oil, whisking constantly until incorporated.

2 Use immediately or cover and refrigerate for up to 2 weeks.

TOBY'S TIP: You can also use this vinaigrette as a marinade for chicken, fish or shrimp. Just combine the ingredients in a large bowl, add the protein and refrigerate for about 30 minutes before cooking.

NUTRITION INFORMATION (PER SERVING)

Calories: 165
Total Fat: 19 g • Saturated Fat: 3 g
Protein: 0 g • Total Carbohydrates: 1 g
Fiber: 0 g • Sugars: 0 g
Sodium: 139 mg • Cholesterol: 0 mg

LIGHTER BUTTERMILK DRESSING

Most store-bought buttermilk dressings are full of saturated fat. This healthier version is just as creamy as the full-fat version, but with a fraction of the calories and artery-clogging fat.

MAKES 8 SERVINGS (1 CUP/250 ML)
SERVING SIZE: ABOUT 2 TBSP (30 ML)

Blender

½ cup (125 mL) low-fat buttermilk

¼ cup (60 mL) light mayonnaise

¼ cup (60 mL) plain nonfat Greek yogurt

2 tsp (10 mL) Worcestershire sauce

1 tsp (5 mL) white wine vinegar

½ tsp (2 mL) garlic powder

¼ tsp (1 mL) dried parsley

¼ tsp (1 mL) salt

⅛ tsp (0.5 mL) ground black pepper

1 In a blender, combine the buttermilk, mayonnaise, Greek yogurt, Worcestershire sauce, white wine vinegar, garlic powder, parsley, salt and pepper; blend on high speed until smooth.

2 Use immediately or transfer to an airtight container, cover and refrigerate for up to 5 days.

NUTRITION INFORMATION (PER SERVING)

Calories: 30
Total Fat: 2 g • Saturated Fat: 0 g
Protein: 1 g • Total Carbohydrates: 2 g
Fiber: 0 g • Sugars: 1 g
Sodium: 173 mg • Cholesterol: 2 mg

CILANTRO-LIME DRESSING

Cilantro is a distinctive and delicious herb that complements many dishes, including Taco Salad (page 144). You can also use it to marinate fish for fish tacos; place 1 pound (500 g) fish in a bowl with the marinade, cover and refrigerate for 30 minutes before cooking.

MAKES 4 SERVINGS (½ CUP/125 ML)
SERVING SIZE: 2 TBSP (30 ML)

2 tbsp (30 mL) freshly squeezed lime juice

2 tbsp (30 mL) chopped fresh cilantro

½ tsp (2 mL) garlic powder

½ tsp (2 mL) ground cumin

¼ tsp (1 mL) salt

⅛ tsp (0.5 mL) ground black pepper

6 tbsp (90 mL) extra-virgin olive oil

1　In a small bowl, whisk together the lime juice, cilantro, garlic powder, cumin, salt and pepper. Slowly drizzle in the olive oil, whisking constantly until incorporated.

2　Use immediately or cover and refrigerate for up to 5 days.

TOBY'S TIP: Extra-virgin olive oil has a distinctive flavor that works well in vinaigrettes, but you can also use regular olive oil, canola oil, avocado oil or safflower oil — which you may already have in your kitchen.

NUTRITION INFORMATION (PER SERVING)

Calories: 185
Total Fat: 21 g • Saturated Fat: 3 g
Protein: 0 g • Total Carbohydrates: 1 g
Fiber: 0 g • Sugars: 0 g
Sodium: 149 mg • Cholesterol: 0 mg

DILL YOGURT DRESSING

Using yogurt in dressings help replace higher-fat ingredients, making them a lower-calorie option. Substitute this version for Lemon Vinaigrette in All Greens Salad (page 122) or Lemon Orzo Salad with Peas and Salmon (page 131).

MAKES 4 SERVINGS (½ CUP/125 ML)
SERVING SIZE: 2 TBSP (30 ML)

Blender

½ cup (125 mL) plain nonfat Greek yogurt

½ medium shallot, roughly chopped

1 tbsp (15 mL) low-fat milk

1 tbsp (15 mL) chopped fresh dill

1 tbsp (15 mL) drained capers

1 tbsp (15 mL) freshly squeezed lemon juice

1　In a blender, combine the Greek yogurt, shallot, milk, dill, capers and lemon juice; blend on high speed until smooth, about 1 minute.

2　Use immediately or cover and refrigerate for up to 1 week.

NUTRITION INFORMATION (PER SERVING)

Calories: 23
Total Fat: 0 g • Saturated Fat: 0 g
Protein: 3 g • Total Carbohydrates: 2 g
Fiber: 0 g • Sugars: 1 g
Sodium: 76 mg • Cholesterol: 2 mg

SESAME GINGER DRESSING

This tangy dressing has a bit of a kick! It can be used on a variety of salads, including Kale and Carrot Salad (page 114) and Soba Noodle Salad with Vegetables and Grilled Tofu (page 128).

MAKES 4 SERVINGS (¼ CUP/60 ML)
SERVING SIZE: 1 TBSP (15 ML)

1½ tbsp (22 mL) reduced-sodium soy sauce

2 tbsp (30 mL) rice wine vinegar

1 tbsp (15 mL) liquid honey or agave nectar

1 tsp (5 mL) Sriracha

¼ tsp (1 mL) ground ginger

3 tbsp (45 mL) extra-virgin olive oil

1 tsp (5 mL) sesame seeds

1 In a small bowl, whisk together the soy sauce, rice wine vinegar, honey, Sriracha and ginger. Slowly drizzle in the olive oil, whisking constantly until incorporated. Add the sesame seeds and whisk to combine.

2 Use immediately or cover and refrigerate for up to 1 week.

TOBY'S TIP: Use tamari instead of soy sauce to make this recipe gluten-free.

NUTRITION INFORMATION (PER SERVING)

Calories: 121
Total Fat: 11 g • Saturated Fat: 1 g
Protein: 1 g • Total Carbohydrates: 7 g
Fiber: 0 g • Sugars: 6 g
Sodium: 167 mg • Cholesterol: 0 mg

TAHINI DRESSING

The main ingredient in this recipe is tahini, a popular Middle Eastern condiment made from toasted sesame seeds. Tahini has a slightly bitter, earthy flavor; the lemon juice adds acidity while the maple syrup adds sweetness. This dressing is delicious!

MAKES 4 SERVINGS (½ CUP/125 ML)
SERVING SIZE: 2 TBSP (30 ML)

¼ cup (60 mL) tahini

¼ cup (60 mL) warm water

2 tbsp (30 mL) freshly squeezed lemon juice

1 tbsp (15 mL) pure maple syrup

1 tbsp (15 mL) sesame oil

¼ tsp (1 mL) garlic powder

¼ tsp (1 mL) salt

1 In a small bowl, whisk together the tahini and water. Add the lemon juice, maple syrup, sesame oil, garlic powder and salt; whisk to combine.

2 Use immediately or cover and refrigerate for up to 1 week.

TOBY'S TIP: Tahini can have too strong a taste for some people. You can always add 2 to 4 tbsp (30 to 60 mL) warm water to make the flavor slightly less intense.

NUTRITION INFORMATION (PER SERVING)

Calories: 130
Total Fat: 11 g • Saturated Fat: 2 g
Protein: 3 g • Total Carbohydrates: 8 g
Fiber: 1 g • Sugars: 4 g
Sodium: 160 mg • Cholesterol: 0 mg

LIGHTER THOUSAND ISLAND DRESSING

The secret ingredient in Thousand Island dressing is sweet pickle relish. All you need is a little bit to punch up the flavor of this dressing. You can find sweet pickle (green) relish in the condiment aisle near the pickles, ketchup and mustard.

MAKES 6 SERVINGS (¾ CUP/175 ML)
SERVING SIZE: ABOUT 2 TBSP (30 ML)

¼ cup (60 mL) plain reduced-fat Greek yogurt

¼ cup (60 mL) light mayonnaise

3 tbsp (45 mL) low-fat milk

1 tbsp (15 mL) ketchup

1 tsp (5 mL) Worcestershire sauce

½ tsp (2 mL) garlic powder

½ tsp (2 mL) Sriracha

¼ tsp (1 mL) salt

1 tbsp (15 mL) sweet pickle relish

1. In a small bowl, whisk together the Greek yogurt, mayonnaise, milk, ketchup, Worcestershire sauce, garlic powder, Sriracha and salt. Stir in the relish until combined.

2. Use immediately or cover and refrigerate for up to 4 days.

TOBY'S TIP: To cut the calories and saturated fat in mayo-based dressings, replace up to half of the mayo with nonfat or reduced-fat Greek yogurt.

NUTRITION INFORMATION (PER SERVING)

Calories: 43
Total Fat: 3 g • Saturated Fat: 1 g
Protein: 1 g • Total Carbohydrates: 4 g
Fiber: 0 g • Sugars: 3 g
Sodium: 243 mg • Cholesterol: 3 mg

CAESAR DRESSING

Here I've modified traditional Caesar dressing, using Greek yogurt in place of some of the mayo, to make it lighter without losing any of the creamy texture.

MAKES 8 SERVINGS (1 CUP/250 ML)
SERVING SIZE: 2 TBSP (30 ML)

¼ cup (60 mL) light mayonnaise

½ cup (125 mL) plain nonfat Greek yogurt

2 tbsp (30 mL) olive oil

2 tbsp (30 mL) freshly squeezed lemon juice

1 tbsp (15 mL) Dijon mustard

1 tsp (5 mL) Worcestershire sauce

¼ cup (60 mL) grated Parmesan cheese

1 tsp (5 mL) garlic powder

⅛ tsp (0.5 mL) ground black pepper

1. In a small bowl, whisk together the mayonnaise, Greek yogurt, olive oil, lemon juice, mustard, Worcestershire sauce, Parmesan cheese, garlic powder and pepper.

2. Use immediately or cover and refrigerate for up to 4 days.

TOBY'S TIP: Swap the olive oil for a mild-flavored oil such as safflower, avocado or canola.

NUTRITION INFORMATION (PER SERVING)

Calories: 74
Total Fat: 6 g • Saturated Fat: 1 g
Protein: 3 g • Total Carbohydrates: 2 g
Fiber: 0 g • Sugars: 1 g
Sodium: 163 mg • Cholesterol: 5 mg

ACKNOWLEDGMENTS

I cannot believe this is my tenth cookbook! Each one I write is a team effort. There are many people I want to thank for making this special book possible. First and foremost, I want to thank my three children, Schoen, Ellena and Micah, for supporting me through this long process and all the recipes you taste-tested. I am proud that all of you love your veggies, and I hope you keep up that healthy habit throughout your lives.

A huge thank you to my literary agent, Sally Ekus from the Ekus Group, who always believed in me. Thanks to Jaimee Constantine and Sara Pokorny from the Ekus Group for your kindness and support throughout the process. Many thanks to Robert Dees from Robert Rose Inc. for believing in me and publishing this project. To my amazing editor, Meredith Dees, thank you for your organization, patience, continued support and guidance throughout this project. I am truly honored to work with an editor who is as talented as you. Thank you to Gillian Watts, Kelly Jones, Rachel Harry and Megan Brush, who all contributed to the book's success. Thanks to Kevin Cockburn for creating the design of this book. Last, thank you to the talented Ashley Lima for being the best food photographer a gal could ask for!

INDEX